A
Guide to Better Spelling

Angela Burt, BA

STANLEY THORNES (PUBLISHERS) LTD

First published in 1982 by
Stanley Thornes (Publishers) Ltd
Old Station Drive
Leckhampton
CHELTENHAM GL53 0DN
England

British Library Cataloguing in Publication Data

Burt, A.M.
  Guide to better spelling
  1. Spellers
  I. Title
  428.1   PE1145.2

ISBN 0-85950-343-7

Reprinted 1982 with amendments
Reprinted 1985
Reprinted 1987

Typeset by Quadraset Ltd, Radstock, Bath
Printed in Great Britain at The Bath Press, Avon

Contents

FOREWORD

Some people seem to be naturally 'good spellers'; many find spelling difficult. This book will be helpful to those who are frequently uncertain how to spell a word, for it has been written with their difficulties in mind.

The book deals with ten basic spelling rules and these are the key to many thousands of words in the language; the book also picks out those words which are commonly misspelt in the work of examination candidates. There are plenty of exercises, dictation passages and revision tests because practice and drill are vital. The user should work steadily and not try to do too much at one time as the work is concentrated and 'a little and often' is good advice in spelling practice. The answers to all the exercises are at the back of the book.

Many users will have to eradicate mistakes which have been repeated for years. It is not easy to break these old habits, but it *can* be done if the user is determined. A student once remarked, 'If there's a right way to spell a word, I want to know it', and that is exactly the attitude to take over spelling improvement.

There has been no attempt to include 'advanced' spellings of a complexity which would daunt the diffident. The intention has been to include words in common usage by the average GCSE candidate and to deal with these as simply and as encouragingly as possible. The spelling of more obscure and demanding words can be checked in a dictionary, and in the examination room such mistakes are not serious. It is the 'high frequency' words which should be mastered first and which present the most urgent need.

Spelling in schools and colleges has in recent years been somewhat neglected, but there is now a growing awareness of its importance. Many examining boards emphasise the need for accurate spelling and candidates may well be penalised for misspelling the kinds of words that are dealt with in this book.

To be able to spell correctly brings undoubted confidence and users of this book will gain in many ways from working through it.

Angela Burt   *Exmouth, 1982*

Spot the Difference

In our language, we have a host of troublesome little words which besiege a student as soon as he puts pen to paper. They come in twos and threes. Some sound the same but are spelt differently; others are pronounced differently but are very similar in the way they are spelt.

There are many students who confess to having guessed quite wildly throughout their school life, unaware that there are logical ways of distinguishing between such words.

It is possible to make your choice an informed one. To assist in this, clear illustrative sentences of the most commonly misspelt pairs (and trios) will be given so that you will receive guidance where needed.

TO, TOO, TWO

To

1) I hope *to* see 'Hamlet'. (= preposition used to form infinitive 'to see')
2) We went *to* Chester. (= preposition suggesting *place* or destination)

Too

1) Are you coming *too*? (= as well)
2) You are *too* fat. (= excessively. Note 'excess' of O's!)

Two

1) It costs *two* pounds. (= £2.00)

EXERCISE 1

Insert TO, TOO, TWO in the correct places. Look back at the illustrative sentences for guidance. Answers to Exercises 1–34 are given on pages 84–7.

1. He wanted _____ go _____ the cinema.
2. It's _____ hot _____ wear a coat.
3. Do you know how _____ do percentages?
4. Maggie hopes _____ 'phone him tomorrow.
5. Will Mrs. Jones come _____?
6. These _____ cases are far _____ heavy.
7. Nobody wants _____ be unfair.
8. Mr. Thorne promised _____ give his permission.

If you have made some mistakes in Exercise 1, you will need to sort them out before trying the next exercise. Once again, refer to the illustrative sentences whenever you need guidance.

EXERCISE 2

Insert TO, TOO, TWO correctly in the following.

1. I _____ enjoy ice-cream.
2. We are _____ excited _____ sleep.
3. _____ young _____ die.
4. _____ cats were seen in the garden.
5. Timothy hopes _____ go _____ University.
6. The shopping bag was _____ flimsy.
7. _____ of us could try _____ contact her.
8. His parents are _____ impatient with him.
9. It's _____ late now.
10. _____ post the parcel will be _____ expensive.
11. He hopes _____ be an architect.
12. It's nine miles _____ Babylon.
13. He will be going _____ Exeter School in September.
14. No one is _____ old _____ learn.

If you are still making mistakes with these words, you are not going to be able to cure yourself overnight. You will need to be very vigilant and to practise regularly until the correct spelling becomes automatic.

Analyse your mistakes carefully. You may find that it is just *one* use of *one* word that you are getting wrong every time.

EXERCISE 3

Insert TO, TOO, TWO.

1. It's ____ hot in here.
2. They're ____ stupid ____ change.
3. The whole class is going ____ London by train.
4. I was told ____ leave the room.
5. Is your father coming ____?
6. Will you go ____ the Post Office for me?
7. The headmaster ____ will be in the classroom.
8. Those cats are ____ lazy ____ move.

EXERCISE 4

Insert TO, TOO, TWO.

1. I've never been ____ a foreign country.
2. Do you know how ____ mend a puncture?
3. This cake is ____ rich for me.
4. There are ____ bicycles for sale.
5. You ____ can be a millionaire.
6. ____ heads are better than one.
7. I hope ____ finish the sweater tonight.
8. All their friends laughed ____.
9. Are you allowed ____ eat sweets if you are a diabetic?
10. Nobody likes ____ be criticised all the time.

Read the following dictation passage very carefully. Pay close attention to the use of TO, TOO and TWO. Look back at the illustrative sentences at the beginning of this section if you are not sure why the chosen form has been used.

3

Ask someone to dictate the passage to you and, without looking again at the passage, see if you can spell every word faultlessly.

PREPARED DICTATION

It was much too hot for my father to mow the lawn although he knew the grass was too long to be left for another two weeks. To my surprise, my mother too said she felt tired. She was going to bed at one point but then sat down to write two letters.

You may have misspelt other words in the passage (apart from TO, TOO and TWO). It would be a very good idea if you were to note down the correct version of every word you misspell as you work your way through this book.

A small alphabetical notebook makes an ideal personal spelling dictionary and every time you use it to check the spelling of a word, you are reinforcing your grasp of that word.

This first section is concentrating on these short, apparently simple words that cause so much trouble. There are not many other tricky words in these short dictations (although SURPRISE and TIRED may have caught some of you out in the passage above). Nevertheless, now is the time to make good resolutions about isolating all the words that you find difficult to spell.

The first step towards improving your spelling is finding out which words you've been getting wrong all your life. Once you have identified them, you can set about learning the correct version.

THERE, THEIR, THEY'RE

There

1) *There* is no hope. ('There is', 'there will be' etc. = impersonal construction.)
2) He ran here and *there*. (= adverb of place. Notice similar spelling of here/there/where = place.)

Their

1) They have lost *their* cat. (= possessive adjective, belonging to them)

They're

1) *They're* late. (= they are (contraction))

EXERCISE 5

Refer back to the illustrative sentences as often as you wish and insert THERE, THEIR, THEY'RE in the spaces below.

1. ____ too ill to come to the party.
2. ____ will be a thunder-storm soon.
3. Have you ever been ____?
4. I believe ____ quite well-known.
5. Suddenly ____ was a loud bang.
6. I know ____ sorry for what happened.
7. They have sold ____ house.
8. At last ____ coming.
9. I'll get over ____ at once.
10. Please go ____ and wait for me.

Look carefully at any mistakes you have made to make sure you will not fall into the same trap again. Try again with the following exercise. Look back at the illustrative sentences; they will guide you.

EXERCISE 6

Insert THERE, THEIR, THEY'RE as appropriate.

1. ____ is no point in arguing.
2. My parents have redecorated ____ kitchen.
3. I've never been ____ before.
4. ____ is no smoke without fire.
5. ____ children are all brilliant.
6. Nobody ____ has ever heard of him.
7. ____ is no point in discussing it.

5

8. Mrs. Greenham is ____ godmother.
9. ____ grandmother was a real character.
10. I know ____ hoping for a visit.

Refresh your memory if you wish before tackling the next two exercises.

EXERCISE 7

Insert THERE, THEIR, THEY'RE. Try not to look back this time.

1. ____ both very sensible.
2. I know ____ mother will be horrified.
3. I love receiving ____ letters.
4. ____ are three possibilities you should consider.
5. I left my bag over ____.
6. ____ answers are always vague.
7. The hikers had lost ____ way.
8. They waited ____ for ten minutes.
9. ____ both coming.
10. ____ will be trouble over this.

EXERCISE 8

Insert THERE, THEIR, THEY'RE. Try not to look back.

1. ____ a nice family.
2. The delegates have made up ____ minds.
3. I know ____ reliable.
4. ____ must have been some mistake.
5. I hope ____ will be an investigation.
6. My neighbours have cancelled ____ papers.
7. ____ always the first to arrive.
8. Do you know ____ telephone number?
9. I put your sweater ____ myself.
10. Have you seen ____ car?

There will be additional practice at the end of this section. Read the following dictation passage very carefully, noting how 'there',

6

'their' and 'they're' have been used. Ask someone to dictate the passage to you and do your best to get every spelling absolutely right without looking.

PREPARED DICTATION

They're going to sell their car at last. Just look at it over there! There is no hope of a quick sale although two people have said that they're quite interested. They're asking too much. I know they're hard up at the moment but there's a limit to what they can do about it, isn't there?

Did you get the following words right?

people　　　*moment*　　　*limit*

PAST, PASSED

Past

1) I am fascinated by the *past*. (= noun)
2) He is a *past* pupil of mine. (= adjective describing 'pupil')
3) He walked *past* me. (= preposition suggesting 'place')
4) He walked *past*. (= adverb of place)

Passed

1) She *passed* me in the High Street. (= verb)
2) She has *passed* me twice. (= verb)

Note　　It is *past* my bedtime.
BUT　　It has *passed* my bedtime.

These last two examples illustrate the most complex of the difficulties associated with this pair of words.

If you are not familiar with grammatical terminology (some simple terms are explained under *Terms You Need To Know* on pages 95–6) and are therefore not helped by it, skip the next paragraph. It is hoped that the illustrative sentences will be enough to guide you when you are uncertain as to which word to use.

For those interested in grammar, 'past' and 'passed' have two quite different functions in the two sentences.

1) *It is past my bedtime.*

It is (subject and verb)

past my bedtime (preposition and adjective and noun = adverbial phrase of time modifying 'is').

2) *It has passed my bedtime.*

It has passed (subject and verb) (verb here = auxiliary verb 'has' and past participle 'passed')

my bedtime (adjective and noun = direct object of 'has passed').

EXERCISE 9

Complete the blanks with PAST or PASSED.

1. The sentry ____ the spot every fifteen minutes.
2. It is half ____ four.
3. It is ____ my lunch hour.
4. What is the ____ tense of this verb?
5. He has a mysterious ____.
6. I've ____ your house every day this week.
7. The ____ is over and forgotten.
8. The thief ran ____ the 'phone box.
9. We ____ the parcel from hand to hand.
10. The train rushed ____ the platform.

Look carefully at any mistakes you have made (remember the answers are on page 84) and make sure you can see where you went wrong.

EXERCISE 10

Insert PAST or PASSED. Look back if you wish.

1. The dog ran ____ the gate.
2. ____ the dairy is a butcher's shop.
3. They ____ him every day.
4. It has ____ six o'clock.
5. It is ____ six o'clock.

8

6. Have you ____ your father the gravy?
7. I ____ you in the Strand this morning.
8. I shall forget the ____ as quickly as I can.
9. Nobody has ____ this spot for one hour.
10. Creep ____ the front door.

EXERCISE 11

Insert PAST or PASSED. Look back if you wish.

1. The bus ____ me at the top of the road.
2. He sauntered ____ the parked car.
3. I should like to know more about his ____.
4. It is a long way ____ lunch-time.
5. My father ____ me a five pound note.
6. I can never go ____ a sweet-shop without going in.
7. His ____ record is excellent.
8. They ____ the hat around.
9. We must have ____ you on the way.
10. I have ____ that page already.

Try to do the following exercise without looking back. By all means, refresh your memory before you start.

EXERCISE 12

PAST or PASSED?

1. We are ____ our prime.
2. The nurse ____ the scalpel to the surgeon.
3. You have ____ your examination.
4. Your ____ offences cannot be disregarded.
5. Hop ____ the apple tree and then run back.
6. I've been listening to the serial for the ____ ten weeks.
7. My boy-friend walked straight ____ me.
8. The little boys ____ the sweets around.
9. My ____ successes are forgotten now.
10. They have already ____ the half-way point.

9

Read the following passage carefully before asking someone to dictate it to you, then, without looking again at the passage, see if you can write it without any spelling error.

PREPARED DICTATION

Brian walked past the cinema. Half-past six. She was late. The crowd streamed past him. He stood still while memories of being let down in the past passed through his mind. He tried to forget the past and looked around him. He was sure that girl over there had passed him once already. Time passed.

Did you spell these words correctly?

memories   *tried*   *already*

ITS and IT'S

Its

1) The dog wagged *its* tail. (= belonging to it (possessive adjective))

It's

1) *It's* a fine day. (= it is (contraction))
2) *It's* been an adventure. (= it has (contraction))

EXERCISE 13

Use ITS or IT'S.

1. _____a pity that you weren't here.
2. The dog scratched _____ ear.
3. The pram has lost _____ wheel.
4. _____ handle has come off.
5. _____ an ill-wind that blows nobody any good.
6. _____ been a long time since I saw you.
7. _____ too late now.
8. The gardener trimmed _____ branches.
9. _____ ears are too long.
10. The boy kicked _____ top off.

10

EXERCISE 14

Use ITS or IT'S.

1. My watch has lost ____ second-hand.
2. I know ____ too late to ask for help.
3. The cat lazily twitched ____ ear.
4. ____ quite clear now.
5. That joke has lost ____ point.
6. Few people really enjoy ____ taste.
7. I'm sorry ____ damaged.
8. ____ been difficult to walk with crutches.
9. Do you know ____ origin?
10. ____ easy if you know what you're doing.

As before, read the passage carefully and then ask someone to dictate it to you.

PREPARED DICTATION

It's a pity your mattress has lost its bounce. Do you think it's anything to do with its age? Perhaps it's not a top quality bed in which case it's lasted quite well. It's not worth repairing it. Its life is over. I know it's a pity.

Did you spell these words correctly?

repairing   *mattress*   *quality*

WERE, WHERE

Were (rhymes with her)

1) We *were* sorry for the mistake. (= past tense of verb 'are')

Where (rhymes with air)

1) *Where* are you going? (= a question to do with 'place' (remember 'here' and 'there'))
2) I know *where* he is. (= again to do with place)
3) The house *where* he lives is beautiful. (= again to do with place)

11

EXERCISE 15

Use WERE or WHERE.

1. _____ did you get that hat?
2. We know _____ you live.
3. The animals _____ shockingly neglected.
4. They _____ very depressed by the news.
5. I know _____ the large plates are.
6. There _____ cobwebs by the sink.
7. _____ is the library?
8. _____ you there?
9. We _____ afraid.
10. Have you any idea _____ we are?

EXERCISE 16

Use WERE or WHERE. Look back at the illustrative sentences if you wish.

1. I don't know _____ it is.
2. _____ you on the bus?
3. He knows _____ you live.
4. The house _____ the road bends is up for sale.
5. We _____ astonished at the news.
6. They _____ present at the time.
7. I know _____ to find it.
8. The bungalow _____ they live is very tiny.
9. _____ are you?
10. The children _____ running down the road.

Try the next exercise without looking back. A high score should give you confidence.

EXERCISE 17

WERE or WHERE? Don't look back.

1. _____ will you live?
2. Do you know _____ my coat is?

12

3. He hasn't told me ____ he works.
4. ____ you sorry?
5. The staff ____ indignant.
6. We ____ hoping to move to the town ____ my son lives.
7. The men ____ repairing the road.
8. ____ does it hurt?
9. The workmen ____ wondering ____ to put it.
10. ____ they there?
11. If I ____ you, I'd forget all about it.
12. We stayed in the house ____ Dickens's daughters ____ born.

Examine your mistakes carefully and make sure you understand where you have been going wrong.

EXERCISE 18

WERE or WHERE? Don't look back.

1. I see now ____ you have been going wrong.
2. I know ____ I would like to go on holiday.
3. All the flags ____ out for the Royal Wedding.
4. That young man knows ____ he wants to go.
5. ____ ____ you on the 29th September?
6. ____ are the snows of yester-year?
7. I wonder who the culprits ____.
8. My neighbours ____ always helpful.
9. ____ you surprised at the news?

Ask someone to dictate the following passage to you. After you have done this, try reading it aloud yourself to see whether you can distinguish between 'were' and 'where'.

PREPARED DICTATION

We were waiting where the path joins the main track. There were no sounds at all and we were all wondering if we had made a mistake. Were we supposed to meet here at six o'clock? Questions were

13

forming mentally but were not voiced. If we were in the right place at the right time, where were the others?

Did you spell these words correctly?
wondering   *voiced*

LOSE, LOOSE

Lose (rhymes with whose)

1) You'll *lose* that wallet. (= verb. Infinitive = to lose.)

Loose (rhymes with goose)

1) I have a *loose* tooth. (= adjective. Remember this phrase. Notice 'oo' repeated.)

EXERCISE 19

Use LOSE or LOOSE.

1. Don't _____ your cheque-book!
2. My belt is too _____.
3. A tooth is painful when it's _____.
4. You'll _____ that pen.
5. I'm afraid the window-frame is rather _____.
6. She's a _____ woman.
7. This tile feels _____.
8. You'll _____ marks for poor punctuation.
9. The _____ wheels were the cause of the accident.
10. _____ paving stones are dangerous.

EXERCISE 20

Use LOSE or LOOSE.

1. She is very _____ limbed.
2. The _____ change jangled in his pocket.
3. That buckle is wearing _____.
4. It is easy to _____ his respect.

14

5. You will _____ your way without a compass.
6. They're at a _____ end in the school holidays.
7. I don't want to _____ your friendship.
8. If you _____ the book, you will have to pay a fine.
9. There is a page _____ in this copy.
10. I am sure he will _____ the case.

First read the dictation passage to yourself and then ask someone to dictate it to you.

PREPARED DICTATION

Peter strapped her case loosely to the roof-rack. Sadly, within two miles, the strap had worked loose and the case fell off. It is not pleasant to lose all your best clothes. Peter found that a loose strap can lose you a pretty girl-friend.

Did you spell these words correctly?

pleasant   *pretty*   *clothes*

AFFECT, EFFECT

Affect

1) Smoking will *affect* your asthma. (= verb. Remember '*A*ffect your *A*sthma'!)

Effect

1) The *effect* was ridiculous. (= noun. Remember 'th*E E*ffect'!)

Note also that 'effect' can be a verb – meaning 'bring about'. e.g. The new boss will effect widespread changes very quickly.

Don't let this use worry you. 'Effect' is not used very often as a verb.

15

EXERCISE 21

Use AFFECT or EFFECT.

1. What will be the ____ of opening on Sundays?
2. We shall all be ____ed by the change.
3. The ____ of the cuts will be disastrous.
4. One ____ of the closure will be increased costs.
5. Nobody who is ____ed by pollen should work here.
6. Will it ____ you at all?
7. The main ____ of reorganisation was a saving.
8. I wonder how the news will ____ his wife.
9. Sunshine has a relaxing ____ on everyone.
10. He is still suffering from the ____s of imprisonment.

EXERCISE 22

Use AFFECT or EFFECT.

1. Prices generally will be ____ed by the rise in the cost of petrol.
2. The sound ____s were marvellous.
3. It ____s me more than it ____s you.
4. The strike will ____ all manufacturing industries.
5. The ____ of the Chancellor's warning was dramatic.
6. She will bear the ____s of an unhappy childhood all her life.
7. Her father seemed quite un____ed by the news.
8. What will the ____ be on your business?
9. Nobody will be more ____ed by the change than I.
10. The long-term ____s of the Act cannot yet be known.

Before asking someone to dictate the following passage to you, read it carefully.

PREPARED DICTATION

Valuable crops have been severely affected by the wet, cold weather. Market gardeners feel the effectiveness of long-range forecasting leaves much to be desired. If they had known in advance what the spring was going to be like, the effects on their pockets could have been reduced. Everyone affected in the South-West (the worst-affected area) will meet in Plymouth next Wednesday.

Did you spell these words correctly?

valuable   *severely*   *Wednesday*

PRACTICE and PRACTISE

These two words 'practice' (noun) and 'practise' (verb) often cause a great deal of confusion. There are four other pairs as well. If you are unsure about the meaning of 'noun' and 'verb', refer to pages 95–6.

Nouns	*Verbs*	
practice	practise	
licence	license	
advice	advise	you can hear the
device	devise	difference in pro-
prophecy	prophesy	nunciation with these.

The rule is that you use 'C' for the nouns, and 'S' for the verbs. Look at the examples below.

Nouns

1) An hour's daily practiCe is essential.
2) You must renew your television licenCe.
3) His adviCe was to go home immediately.
4) There was an intricate deviCe on the back.
5) The politician's propheCy was a gloomy one.

Verbs (including past and present participles)

1) Dr. Green has practiSed in Exmouth for thirty years.
2) Is this a licenSed restaurant? (past participle)
3) We are adviSing you to go abroad. (present participle)
4) I must deviSe a solution to this tricky problem.
5) The preacher propheSied the end of the world this century.

If the grammatical basis of this rule doesn't help you, use advice/advise, device/devise as a touchstone. You can *hear* the difference in spelling with these words.

EXERCISE 23

1. Matthew ____s every day at the piano. (practice, practise)
2. You will need a ____ for that dog. (licence, license)
3. You have to ____ a public house for singing and dancing. (licence, license)
4. ____ makes perfect. (practice, practise)
5. The Government ____s all householders to insulate their roofs. (advice, advise)
6. The ____ came true. (prophecy, prophesy)
7. Why ____ such a dreadful end for the human race? (prophecy, prophesy)
8. Have you any ____ to offer me? (advice, advise)
9. Did you really ____ this little scheme? (device, devise)
10. With ____, your work will improve. (practice, practise)

EXERCISE 24

Use PRACTICE or PRACTISE.

1. An hour's ____ is not enough.
2. Gymnasts must ____ every day.
3. I wonder if he will ____ what he preaches.
4. Regular ____ is essential.
5. The doctor's ____ was a scattered one.
6. You will be able to do it with ____.
7. In ____ the idea is hopeless.
8. The cast will ____ the dance every day.
9. The little girl loathes her piano ____.
10. ____ standing on your head. It will relax you!

EXERCISE 25

Use LICENCE or LICENSE.

1. You will need a ____.

2. Have you renewed your television ____?
3. Is it necessary to ____ such premises?
4. The ____ is very expensive.
5. The ____ costs five pounds.
6. You must renew your ____ by the 30th June.
7. His ____ has nearly expired.
8. He tore the ____ in two very angrily.
9. We hope we can ____ the club for singing and dancing.
10. A current driving ____ is essential.

The following dictation passage should be read before asking someone to dictate it to you.

PREPARED DICTATION

What advice can I give you? You know you need a separate licence to serve wine and spirits and your restaurant is at the moment unlicensed. Others will advise you to apply for a licence but I cannot prophesy much success. You will need to practise great patience and would be better advised to devise some other way of making your fortune.

Did you spell these words correctly?

separate   *restaurant*   *patience*

EIGHTEEN FURTHER EXAMPLES

I have dealt at some length with the groups of words that cause the most widespread confusion. However, I know only too well that individual students will have trouble with other pairs as well. I have listed some of these below and I hope the brief clues and the illustrative sentences will be a help.

1. ACCEPT (= receive)	e.g. I *accept* your gift with pleasure.
EXCEPT	e.g. Everyone *except* James can come.

19

2. ALLOWED (= permitted) e.g. You are not *allowed* to smoke.

   ALOUD e.g. He laughed *aloud*.

3. BEECH (= tree) e.g. The *beech* tree is magnificent.

   BEACH e.g. Let's sunbathe on the *beach*.

4. BORED (= not interested) e.g. He is *bored* by the subject.

   BOARD e.g. You need some *board* 20 cm × 30 cm.

5. BUY (= purchase) e.g. I shall *buy* myself a bikini.
   BY e.g. The message is *by* the 'phone.

6. CLOTHES (= garments) e.g. We all enjoy wearing new *clothes*.

   CLOTHS e.g. You need soft *cloths* for polishing.

7. MEAT (= food) e.g. *Eat* your *meat*.
   MEET e.g. *Meet* me at six o'clock.

8. NEW (= not old) e.g. My son wants a *new* bicycle.

   KNEW e.g. I *knew* it would *k*ick.

9. NO (= not any
        = opposite of YES) e.g. I can offer *no* hope.

   KNOW e.g. Do you *know* the answer?

10. OF (pronounced OV) e.g. She is a mother *of* five.
    OFF e.g. Keep *off* the grass.

11. QUIET (= not noisy) e.g. Please be *quiet* for a moment.

    QUITE e.g. You are really *quite* clever.

20

12. SEAM (= joined edges of material)   e.g. You must sew that *seam* again.

SEEM   e.g. It would *seem* he has left.

13. SURE (= certain)   e.g. I am *sure* he will come.

SHORE   e.g. The sea*shore* is fascinating.

14. THREW (= hurled)   e.g. He *threw* the ball.

THROUGH   e.g. We walked *through* the park.

15. WHOLE (= entire)   e.g. The bridegroom ate the *whole* wedding cake.

HOLE   e.g. You have a *hole* in your *h*at.

16. WEATHER (= climate)   e.g. The *weather* is so wintry for Easter.

WHETHER   e.g. I don't know *whether* Louise will be coming. *Whether* you win or lose is really unimportant.

17. WHO'S (= who is, who has)   e.g. *Who's* there?

   e.g. *Who's* been using my lipstick?

WHOSE   e.g. *Whose* book is that?

   e.g. You are the man *whose* cat has died.

18. YOU'RE (= you are)   e.g. *You're* very kind.

YOUR   e.g. Please collect *your* belongings.

ONE WORD OR TWO?

The following words can be one word or two words depending on meaning.

1) He is *also* a scout.

1) They were *all so* happy.

21

2) Have you eaten *already?*	2) Are you *all ready* to go?
3) We *always do* this.	3) These are *all ways* into town.
4) It is *altogether* too difficult.	4) We found them *all together.*
5) He *almost* fell.	5) They were *all most* helpful.
6) I shall come *anyway.*	6) I cannot think of *any way.*
7) *Sometimes* I go to London.	7) There are *some times* when life seems hard.

Remember: *SPEAK* (you speak well) but *SPEECH* (your speech was very effective).

REVISION TEST

(Total Marks = 100)

EXERCISE 26

Insert as appropriate.

1. Will you come _____? (to, too, two)
2. I am _____ tired _____ sleep. (to, too, two)
3. I have lost _____ address. (there, their, they're)
4. _____ both feeling much better. (there, their, they're)
5. Are you sneezing _____? (to, too, two)
6. _____ has been an accident. (there, their, they're)
7. Will you be going _____ Exeter? (to, too, two)
8. I should like _____ copies. (to, too, two)
9. I will see you _____. (there, their, they're)

EXERCISE 27

Insert appropriate words as indicated.

1. He goes _____ far. (to, too, two)
2. It's _____ cold _____ go swimming now. (to, too, two)
3. Is your mother coming _____? (to, too, two)

4. He ____ me on the stairs. (past, passed)
5. ____ is no-one in the house. (there, their, they're)
6. My neighbours love ____ garden. (there, their, they're)
7. ____ in Gibraltar for a year. (there, their, they're)
8. Do you know how ____ drive a car? (to, too, two)
9. Have you ever been ____? (there, their, they're)

EXERCISE 28

Use an appropriate word from the brackets.

1. The plans have now been officially ____. (past, passed)
2. Andrew has gone ____ a friend's house. (to, too, two)
3. The motorist drove ____ fast in the fog. (to, too, two)
4. All ____ pupils of the school have been invited. (past, passed)
5. They intend ____ emigrate. (to, too, two)
6. ____ so relieved at the news. (there, their, they're)
7. Dorothy ____ by with her nose in the air. (past, passed)
8. ____ has been a dreadful mistake. (there, their, they're)
9. Anna has ____ her Grade 5 ballet exam. (past, passed)
10. Your work over the ____ year has been excellent. (past, passed)

EXERCISE 29

Use appropriate words from those in brackets.

1. ____ never ____ late ____ learn ____ spell. (its, it's, to, too, two)
2. ____ such a pity ____ leaving London. (its, it's, there, their, they're)
3. ____ both hoping for promotion. (there, their, they're)
4. ____ always a race against time in the garden. (its, it's)
5. I ____ old Mr. Jones in town this morning. (past, passed)
6. I'm afraid ____ ____ expensive for me. (its, it's, to, too, two)
7. A cat values ____ independence. (its, it's)
8. ____ accuracy cannot be guaranteed. (its, it's)
9. Dr. Donald knows ____ parents quite well. (there, their, they're)
10. He has ____ all his papers to me. (past, passed)

EXERCISE 30

Insert as indicated.

1. This exercise is _____ difficult for me. (to, too, two)
2. Your _____ experience is valuable to us. (past, passed)
3. _____ you present on the first night? (were, where)
4. They have crashed _____ car. (there, their, they're)
5. _____ have you been since supper? (were, where)
6. I don't want _____ _____ all my teeth. (to, too, two, lose, loose)
7. We _____ horrified at the news. (were, where)
8. Something is _____ in the engine. (lose, loose)
9. We will _____ the trail if it starts raining. (lose, loose)

EXERCISE 31

Insert TO, TOO, TWO.

1. I still have some ironing _____ do.
2. They are going _____ Cheltenham.
3. The sea is _____ rough _____ go sailing.
4. Marion has broken _____ ribs.
5. Are you learning _____ distinguish between them?
6. It is not easy _____ break a long-established habit.
7. I hope these exercises are not _____ difficult.
8. You _____ can score 100% with care.
9. You are beginning _____ master your difficulties.

EXERCISE 32

Use AFFECT or EFFECT.

1. Every tax-payer will be _____ed by the Budget.
2. How severe will the _____ of the measures be?
3. We will not know the full _____ until next April.
4. The staff will, in _____, be cut by half.
5. This method is very _____ive.
6. I had no idea she would be so _____ed by the news.
7. The visual _____ was stunning.
8. The _____s of your decision will be with us for a long time.

9. Sponge the ____ed area with diluted vinegar.
10. She is a very ____ionate child.

EXERCISE 33

Use an appropriate word from those in brackets.

1. I must ____ more regularly. (practice, practise)
2. ____ many late nights are bad for you. (to, too, two)
3. The letter was ____ heavy for a 14p stamp. (to, too, two)
4. ____ travelling ____ Portsmouth by train. (there, their, they're, to, too, two)
5. In ____ weeks, ____ been ____ much for me. (past, passed, its, it's, to, too, two)
6. ____ did you find it? (were, where)
7. He cannot find the ____ anywhere. (licence, license)

EXERCISE 34

Insert appropriate words as indicated.

1. What beautiful ____ you have! (clothes, cloths)
2. I will give you the best ____ them. (of, off)
3. I was ____ sorry when she left. (quiet, quite)
4. The children went out ____ ____ ____ presents. (to, too, two, buy, by, there, their, they're)
5. Her father ____ all would be well. (new, knew)
6. It would ____ to be a good idea. (seam, seem)
7. Are you ____ ____ you will have time? (quiet, quite, sure, shore)
8. ____ afraid of Virginia Woolf? (who's, whose)
9. ____ absolutely right. (you're, your)
10. Can you find ____ way ____ the maze? (you're, your, threw, through)
11. I ____ the tour well. (no, know)

25

SECTION TWO

Plurals

We shall deal first with the rules governing the formation of plural nouns. Most are very straightforward. Learn the rules thoroughly and then work through the exercises that follow. There is a check list of spellings on pages 88–94 which you can use in marking your work. If you score badly in an exercise, turn back to the rule and study it attentively before working through the exercise again. There are revision exercises at the end of the section.

REGULAR PLURALS

Rule 1	The regular plural of nouns is formed by adding —S to the singular.

Examples

tableS	doorS	bicycleS	sizeS
chairS	ceilingS	bookS	houseS
windowS	floorS	gardenS	roseS

Notice —S with some verbs too:

he lookS	he eatS	he sleepS	it rainS
she fearS	she wakeS	she wonderS	it seemS

NOUNS ENDING IN SIBILANTS

Remember here to *listen* carefully to the word in both the singular and the plural form.

<table>
<tr><td>

Rule 2
</td><td>
Nouns ending in a sibilant (hissing sound) form their plural by adding −ES.
</td></tr>
</table>

You are adding a **syllable** and you can *hear* this if you say the word aloud. (If the sibilant is followed by an −E, as in size, house and rose, refer to Rule 1.)

Examples

s	x	z	ch	sh	tch
classES	taxES	waltzES	archES	flushES	stitchES
atlasES	hoaxES	fezES	porchES	wishES	latchES
busES	boxES		benchES	squashES	hutchES

Notice −ES also after sibilants in verbs:

she dressES	it buzzES	he washES
he fixES	he wrenchES	he watchES

Exercise based on Rule 1 and Rule 2

Do the following exercise without looking back at the two rules.

EXERCISE 35

Complete the following by adding −S or −ES

1. Few people enjoy paying rate__ and tax__.
2. We had eight hen__ eaten by fox__.
3. They are carrying out a survey of the church__ and the chapel__ in the neighbourhood.
4. Clock__ and watch__ need regular cleaning.
5. The conductor__ on the bus__ were very helpful.
6. He wish__ he could pass all the test__.
7. We shall need six new dish__ and eleven new glass__ for our guest__.
8. Robert express__ himself very clearly.
9. Could you pack away the bench__?
10. The rabbit hutch__ are in a dreadful state.
11. Have you seen the proud way she push__ her doll's pram?

27

12. The box__ of firework__ were quite damp.
13. His hunch__ were not always reliable.
14. See how he wrench__ and twist__ that handle!
15. Do you believe in witch__?

When you have checked your work by referring to the check list on pages 88–94, look again at any mistakes you may have made. Remember you can always *hear* the extra syllable made by adding −ES to a word. If ever you are in doubt as to whether you need −S or −ES, *say the plural word to yourself and listen carefully.*

These two rules will be tested again in the dictation passage which follows and also in the revision exercises which conclude the section on plurals.

The basic spelling rules studied in this book are often concerned with the endings of words (as are Rules 1 and 2). However, you may find other parts of the words tricky as well and this is where you simply must learn each word by heart.

Many words which are frequently misspelt have been deliberately incorporated into the dictation passages within this section and are given in the spelling lists preceding each dictation. Study each list carefully before asking someone to dictate the relevant passage to you. There will be other words which you will get wrong—do not let the opportunity of learning the correct version slip past.

Can you spell these?

1. across	5. quiet	9. forty	13. Wednesday
2. heard	6. whether	10. front	14. lose
3. meant	7. behind	11. among	15. because
4. until	8. Tuesday	12. before	16. extremely

Read carefully the following dictation passage. It will test your understanding of Rules 1 and 2 and also your grasp of the spelling list above. Study any other words in the passage that you know you might get wrong.

Home students can perhaps record the passage (at dictation speed!) and then write it out, or perhaps find a friend or relation willing to read the passage aloud to them. School and college students will have a teacher or lecturer at hand!

PREPARED DICTATION

It was extremely dark. Bushes and ferns leant menacingly across the path in front of him, and he heard furtive rustlings and quiet squeaks among the leaves and grasses behind him. He felt tired until he realised it would take him only forty minutes now to reach her cottage if he did not lose his way. He meant to arrive before Tuesday was over; Wednesday would be too late because a solemn promise would have been broken. Until he knocked on that lonely door, he would not know whether she too had kept her word. He hurried forward.

NOUNS ENDING IN −Y

Next comes a most useful rule. It looks complicated when formulated but it is well worth studying it carefully. Errors in the formation of the plural of words ending in Y are very common indeed in the work of GCSE candidates, and are easily avoided. There is only one very minor exception to this rule as you will see.

Consider these words:

boy	boyS	hobby	hobbIES
alley	alleyS	century	centurIES
day	dayS	body	bodIES
buoy	buoyS	baby	babIES
key	keyS	lady	ladIES
guy	guyS	quality	qualitIES
ray	rayS	city	citIES
turkey	turkeyS	party	partIES

What has happened in the formation of the plural? What is the difference between the first list in the singular and the second list? We can formulate Rule 3 as follows:

	(a)	If there's a vowel before the final —**Y**, just add —**S** to form the plural.
Rule 3		**Example:** chimney chimneys
	(b)	If there's a consonant before the final −**Y**, change **Y** to **I** before adding −**ES**.
		Example: opportunity opportunit**IES**

Note: If you are not sure what is meant by 'vowels' and 'consonants' or by any other term used in this book, refer to *'Terms You Need To Know'* on pages 95−6.

EXERCISE 36

Form the plural of the following. (Look back at the rule as often as you wish. It will not let you down!)

1. pony	5. ally	8. attorney
2. turkey	6. library	9. alloy
3. lady	7. baby	10. activity
4. valley		

EXERCISE 37

Form the plural of the following. Try not to look back this time.

1. enemy	5. gipsy	8. lorry
2. kidney	6. quay	9. abbey
3. story	7. ecstasy	10. eccentricity
4. trolley		

Check your work on the above exercises, and all subsequent exercises, by referring to the check list on pages 88−94.

Even if a word is unfamiliar, you will have found you can form its plural safely. We shall have to consider the minor exception in a moment but try just one more exercise first.

Helpful Hint: Remember 'boy/boys' as a memory key to Rule 3. You know already how to spell 'boys' and so you can deduce that all other words ending in a vowel + **Y** will behave in the same way.

You then know it's 'the other lot' that ends in −IES!

EXERCISE 38

Form the plural.

1. jelly	5. laboratory	8. party
2. jersey	6. city	9. jockey
3. factory	7. navy	10. quality
4. puppy		

The only exception is this: the plurals of *proper* nouns ending in a consonant + Y are formed simply by adding −S. This keeps the name intact and therefore recognisable. This is shown in the following examples.

1. There were three MARYS in the class. (Mary Gillespie, Mary Hunt and Mary Rowden)
2. There were two MARIES. (Marie Clancy & Marie Greenham)
3. We saw the HARDYS last night. (i.e. Mr. & Mrs. Hardy)
4. They invited the HARDIES to supper (i.e. Mr. & Mrs. Hardie)

Check your understanding of Rule 3 by completing the following exercise *without referring back*.

EXERCISE 39

1. The (opportunity) that exist are endless.
2. There were two (sentry) on duty.
3. Boys who are (bully) are always unpopular.
4. The hills and (valley) are covered in mist.
5. There is a network of (alley) behind the houses.
6. I don't think they should experiment on (monkey).
7. The new school has splendid (facility) for craftwork.
8. Six (century) ago, few of us would have had glass in our windows.
9. France and Great Britain were (ally) in the last war.
10. We apologise for the (delay).

31

11. Our new house has three (storey).
12. I should enjoy a holiday exploring the (estuary) of the rivers of Devon.
13. There are several (mystery) surrounding that particular light-house.
14. Do you know how many (county) there are in Northern Ireland?
15. I like houses with (balcony).

This rule will also help with verbs.

Vowel + Y

Examples

she enjoyS	he payS	he delayS
she buyS	she employS	he betrayS

Consonant + Y

Examples

he trIES (to try)	she worrIES (to worry)
he qualifIES (to qualify)	it applIES (to apply)

The following exercise is concerned with *verbs* ending in −Y.

EXERCISE 40

Write out the correct form of the present tense.

1. He (employ) ten men.
2. My mother always (buy) too much wool when she knits a sweater.
3. He (deny) ever having met her.
4. That donkey (bray) whenever he sees me.
5. He (worry) unnecessarily about his son.
6. He always (pay) his fare.
7. Do you think he really (try) to do his homework?
8. When Matthew (qualify), he will be twenty-four.
9. You never think that particular rule (apply) to you.
10. The landlord (supply) all linen except tea towels.
11. He (fortify) his house as if it were going to be attacked.
12. My neighbour always (enjoy) 'Panorama'.
13. My godfather (journey) through Europe every year.

14. Her fiancé (study) every weekday evening.
15. Have you noticed that Mr. Jolliffe always (carry) a rolled umbrella?

Can you spell these words?

1. shining
2. probably
3. families
4. excited
5. annual
6. Britain
7. certain
8. beautifully
9. similar
10. pleasant
11. mischievous
12. frightened
13. exhausted
14. occasion
15. exercising
16. Saturday

Read the word list carefully before asking someone to dictate the following passage to you. All the words listed are used in the dictation passage.

PREPARED DICTATION

On a certain Saturday in August the sun was shining. Ponies, beautifully groomed, were exercising in the main ring, crowds wandered through the vegetable tent, and frightened babies cried as turkeys gobbled and donkeys brayed. Exhausted families and parties of excited, mischievous school-children picnicked among the daisies. Always a pleasant occasion, the eighth Annual County Show (probably similar to many others all over Britain) was in progress.

NOUNS ENDING IN −O

We come now to those words which in the singular end in −O. The confusion arises because some form their plural by adding −S, others by adding −ES.

It is easier to remember that most simply add −S but that there are twenty-three words which must end in −ES in the plural. It is worth learning these exceptions.

> **Rule 4** Most nouns ending in −O form their plural by adding −S.

These *include*:

1. Nouns of Spanish and Italian origin and musical nouns.

Examples

sombreroS   soloS   ponchoS

2. Abbreviated nouns.

Examples

photoS   discoS

3. Nouns ending in a double vowel.

Examples

studioS   iglooS

Exceptions

Must be −ES

An asterisk indicates the words you are likely to want most frequently.

*1. buffaloES	*9. heroES	*17. potatoES
2. calicoES	10. innuendoES	18. stuccoES
*3. cargoES	11. jingoES	*19. tomatoES
4. desperadoES	12. mangoES	*20. tornadoES
5. dingoES	*13. mosquitoES	*21. torpedoES
*6. dominoES	*14. NegroES	22. vetoES
*7. echoES	15. noES	*23. volcanoES
8. embargoES	16. peccadilloES	

There is also a group of words which can end either in −OS or −OES, so with these you can never be wrong! Use whichever ending you think looks right but be prepared to see either ending in your reading.

Can be −S or −ES

1. archipelagos   or   archipelagoES
2. bravadoS   or   bravadoES

3. EskimoS	or	EskimoES
4. flamingoS	or	flamingoES
5. frescoS	or	frescoES
6. grottoS	or	grottoES
7. haloS	or	haloES
8. mementoS	or	mementoES
9. mottoS	or	mottoES
10. placeboS	or	placeboES
11. provisoS	or	provisoES
12. stilettoS	or	stilettoES
13. zeroS	or	zeroES

Note: The plural of librettO is librettI

virtuosO is virtuosI.

EXERCISE 41

All the words in this exercise form their plural by adding −S. Look again at the rule and see if you can find out why. (The explanation that will fit one of the words is that it is not included in the list of twenty-three exceptions. The other words all fit into the specific categories mentioned in the rule.)

1. zoo	5. 'cello	8. kangaroo
2. lasso	6. cuckoo	9. shampoo
3. tattoo	7. banjo	10. photo
4. radio		

EXERCISE 42

Do the same with this exercise. Some words may be unfamiliar but the rule will not let you down.

1. scenario	5. magneto	8. cameo
2. contralto	6. patio	9. soprano
3. portfolio	7. casino	10. rodeo
4. trio		

EXERCISE 43

Form the plural of the following. Some exceptions are included.

1. albino
2. biro
3. hippo
4. buffalo
5. kimono
6. domino
7. Negro
8. hero
9. embryo
10. oratorio

Revise the rule very carefully at this stage and memorise it (and the exceptions you need). There will be further revision exercises on this rule at the end of the section but the next exercise could serve as intermediate revision if you try to do it from memory.

EXERCISE 44

Form the plural of the words in brackets.

1. We saw (cargo) of (tomato) and (potato) being unloaded at Portsmouth.
2. Do (Eskimo) really live in (igloo)?
3. Our visit to the television (studio) was very exciting.
4. Lava was pouring from both (volcano).
5. A mock raid by (commando) followed the gymnastic display.
6. The parties' (manifesto) were delivered a week before the election.
7. He has a fine collection of (curio).
8. I always enjoy reading the (motto) in crackers.
9. They slouched along wearing (poncho) and (sombrero).
10. He has built three (gazebo) already.
11. The (soprano) and (contralto) will have an extra rehearsal on Sunday.
12. (Echo) of Laura's voice gradually died away.
13. Purbrook High School now has three (piano).
14. Keep both coins as (memento) of your visit.
15. We were badly bitten by (mosquito).

Two spelling lists follow (study them carefully) and two passages for dictation. The two dictation passages form a continuous narrative and may be joined if time permits. Ask someone to dictate one or both passages to you.

Can you spell these words?

1. embarrassing
2. surprised
3. received
4. accommodation
5. thoroughly
6. February
7. language
8. ghastly
9. island
10. restaurant
11. holiday
12. luxury
13. Mediterranean
14. disappointing
15. really
16. could've (not 'could of')

1. decided
2. truly
3. finally
4. success
5. probably
6. coming
7. preferred
8. I'm
9. suggestion
10. wonder
11. quite
12. abroad

PREPARED DICTATION

We've just received the photos we took on the holiday island in the Mediterranean in February. The embarrassing one of us in sombreros and ponchos will amuse you. The one of the restaurant brings back awful memories of the disappointing food. We were surprised how really ghastly vegetables in olive oil can be, especially potatoes and tomatoes! The weather was thoroughly depressing, our luxury accommodation could've been better, and we had the usual language problems.

However, I'm glad we finally decided to follow your suggestion of going by sea. The journey out there was a great success, although coming back was another matter. The children went to different discos almost every night but we preferred the classical concerts. The oboes and 'cellos were truly magnificent and the singing was really quite breathtaking. The sopranos and contraltos were probably the best I've ever heard. We've kept the beautiful programmes as mementoes. I wonder if we'll go abroad again.

Note: 'Oboes' is the plural of 'oboE' hence −OES.

37

NOUNS ENDING IN −F and −FE

This is a beautifully simple rule with which to end this section and the exceptions are easy because your ear is the guide.

Rule 5	Nouns ending in −F and −FE add −S to form the plural.

Examples

bailiff	—	bailiffs	giraffe	— giraffes
belief	—	beliefs	handkerchief	— handkerchiefs
roof	—	roofs	safe	— safes

Exceptions

There are thirteen exceptions to this rule but don't be alarmed. You can always *hear* −VES.

wives	knives	lives
calves	halves	
elves	selves	shelves
leaves	sheaves	
loaves		
thieves		
wolves		

There are four words which can be spelt either −FS or −VES. Use whichever spelling you prefer but be prepared to see both versions in your reading.

hoofs or hooves   scarfs or scarves
turfs or turves   wharfs or wharves

Note that the verb forms tend to be regular −FS or −FES even when the noun forms are −VES.

1) He kniFES his victim.   2) Clean the kniVES and forks.
3) She leafS through the book. 4) The leaVES are falling.

If in doubt about F or V, say the word aloud and listen carefully. (You may have to learn to pronounce the words correctly in one or

38

two cases. Not everybody says 'roofs' and 'handkerchiefs' properly!)

EXERCISE 45

Form the plural of the following. Look back at the rule if you wish.

1. wife	5. proof	8. flagstaff
2. carafe	6. dwarf	9. knife
3. cliff	7. cast-off	10. chief
4. half		

EXERCISE 46

Form the plural of the following. Trust your ear this time and look back only if you really must.

1. bailiff	5. giraffe	8. tariff
2. life	6. café	9. sheriff
3. herself	7. muff	10. gulf
4. hoof		

Treat this next exercise as a revision exercise. Make sure you understand Rule 5 completely before attempting the exercise from memory.

EXERCISE 47

Form the plural of the words in brackets.

1. A pack of (wolf) was slinking through the shadows.
2. Meat and other (foodstuff) have increased in price.
3. My aunt sent me a box of lace-edged (handkerchief).
4. Foreign ships were unloading at the (wharf).
5. The laughing girls were wearing long football (scarf).
6. The cows were standing contentedly in the field with their (calf).
7. The deserted cottages were without (roof).
8. His (shelf) were loaded with books.
9. Some beautiful fish live on coral (reef).
10. The (thief) ransacked the neat house.

Can you spell these words?

1. quarrelled
2. addressed
3. advisers
4. definite
5. necessary
6. government
7. busily
8. emergency
9. apology
10. already
11. Parliamentary
12. intentions
13. business
14. ninety
15. recognising
16. extraordinary

The following passage makes use of the word list above. Study the list carefully then ask someone to dictate the passage to you.

PREPARED DICTATION

The King of the Dwarfs had quarrelled bitterly with the King of the Elves and there was already a definite threat of war if an apology was not received by Wednesday. The King addressed his chief Parliamentary advisers, warning them of his intentions. It was decided immediately that wives and children should be evacuated and all but necessary business be suspended. Extraordinary emergency plans were drawn up, roofs of government buildings were reinforced, and ninety cannon were hastily erected on cliffs and wharves. The chiefs themselves busily planned the defence of principal cities, recognising that lives were in danger.

REVISION TEST

Now we come to the revision test consisting of five exercises, marked out of 100, which should be done from memory. It will offer a good indication of your understanding and retention of the rules that have been discussed. Remember that you can check your answers to all exercises in this workbook by reference to the check list on pages 88–94.

EXERCISE 48

Form the plural.

1. sinus
2. scratch
3. penalty

4. himself
5. radio
6. volley
7. peony
8. oaf
9. wallaby
10. necessity
11. elf
12. avocado
13. cavy
14. cargo
15. tattoo
16. envoy
17. crutch
18. echo
19. loaf
20. vanity

EXERCISE 49

Form the plural.

1. calf
2. hippopotamus
3. moustache
4. half
5. Christmas
6. secretary
7. pulley
8. abscess
9. understudy
10. empress
11. sheath
12. sheaf
13. city
14. knife
15. memo
16. potato
17. thief
18. pinch
19. chorus
20. hero

EXERCISE 50

Form the plural.

1. mix
2. relay
3. mosquito
4. duty
5. shako
6. ruff
7. leaf
8. piccolo
9. waif
10. lynx
11. volcano
12. galaxy
13. torpedo
14. heiress
15. shelf
16. opportunity
17. mass
18. travesty
19. glass
20. risotto

EXERCISE 51

Write out the correct form of the present tense.

1. A policeman (witness) such things every day.
2. Marilyn (sniff) so loudly.
3. My sister (cry) whenever she falls over.
4. It (terrify) me that he is allowed to drive.

5. Have you seen how the water (eddy) at that point?
6. She (embellish) all her anecdotes.
7. He (punch) you very roughly.
8. You say he (annoy) you with his attention?
9. I can't bear the way she (gush) over animals.
10. Mark (rely) on you for moral support.
11. Thomas Hardy (portray) a man at the mercy of his passions.
12. If he (delay) too long, he will lose his chance.
13. Lydia (try) very hard and her work is improving.
14. The plaintiff (deny) ever having met the witness.
15. Watch how he (leaf) through those letters!
16. Meat soon (putrefy) in a hot climate.
17. The farmer's son (coax) his horse over the fence.
18. Mrs. Brown (envy) everyone.
19. Wisely she (apply) for every post advertised.
20. It (depress) me to see him losing hope.

EXERCISE 52

Form the plural.

1. Christmas	8. entry	15. butterfly
2. battery	9. innuendo	16. trolley
3. yo-yo	10. society	17. bush
4. emissary	11. guest	18. princess
5. lorry	12. idiocy	19. fantasy
6. watch	13. quantity	20. dream
7. panto	14. ogre	

Remember that a thorough mastery of spelling rules will enable you to spell correctly vast numbers of words. Make sure you are thoroughly familiar with the five rules in this section.

Prefixes

GENERAL RULES AND CAUTIONS

Adding prefixes (syllables at beginning of words) to a base word is normally a very straightforward affair and so this section will be a very short one.

Vowels

Prefixes ending in a vowel never change before a base word, nor do they cause a change of spelling in the base word.

Examples

Ashore   DEvote   BIcycle   PREpare

Consonants

1) Most prefixes ending in a consonant don't change.

Examples

EXport   OUTfit   POSTgraduate   UNkind

2) A few prefixes ending in a consonant change for the sake of euphony (pleasantness of sound).

Examples

AD can become:

ACuse	AFfect	AGgravate
ALlocate	ANnounce	APpear
ARrange	ASsemble	AMmunition

CON can become:

COLlect	COMbine	CO-operate
CORrect		

43

DIS can become:

DIFferent

SUB can become:

SUCcumb   SUFfix   SUGgest

IN can become:

IGnore   ILliterate   IMmature
IRregular

There is listed above only one example of each of the changes that can take place. You will notice a chameleon-like change in the last letter of the prefix; the last letter of the prefix can become the same as the first letter of the word to which it is joined.

3) In some cases, the last letter of the prefix and the first letter of the base word are the same anyway and care must be taken to make sure that both are included.

Examples

MISspelling   WITHhold   UNDERrate
Beware the exception   PAStime (not pasttime).

4) Notice that if ALL is used as a prefix, it has only one L.

Examples

aLso   aLready   aLthough   aLways

BUT
ALL RIGHT is always two words.

Note: Be careful to ensure you always write these phrases as two words and not as one:

a lot   in front   in fact
all right   thank you

5) The prefix DIS– never has a double S. Of course, if the DIS– prefix is added to a base word beginning with an S you will have two S's together.

44

Examples

DISappoint   DISingenuous   DISquiet

But

DIS̲satisfy   DIS̲semination

EXERCISE 53

Form the opposites of these words by using the prefixes IN−, UN−, DIS−.

1. disputable
2. credit
3. correct
4. decided
5. formal
6. similar
7. adequate
8. controlled
9. agree
10. co-operative

EXERCISE 54

Form the opposites of these words too, using the prefixes IN−, UN−, DIS−.

1. diluted
2. kind
3. active
4. decisive
5. able
6. ability
7. conclusive
8. direct
9. natural
10. eligible
11. definite
12. predictable
13. fair
14. sophisticated
15. related
16. arrange
17. please
18. tidy
19. visible
20. appear

EXERCISE 55

Form the opposite of these words by using the prefixes IM−, IG−, IR−, IL−.

1. polite
2. relevant
3. mature
4. noble
5. regular
6. mortal
7. literate
8. rational
9. legible
10. resolute
11. responsible
12. mobile
13. pious
14. legal
15. replaceable

EXERCISE 56

Use an appropriate prefix to complete the following.

1. Try to dispel your __judices.
2. I should like you to sit in a __circle facing me.
3. The sky became very __cast.
4. We shall __come our enemy.
5. The headmaster was seriously __pleased.
6. Sebastian spoke his thoughts __loud.
7. It is too late now to __vert disaster.
8. We were __appointed when the parcel didn't arrive.
9. The small boat ran __ground.
10. How __hevelled your hair looks.
11. Both girls will come __though they are tired.
12. The Bank will __hold payment of the cheque.
13. I noticed three __spellings in your work.
14. You __rate his ability.
15. Simon __ways writes an interesting essay.

Can you spell these words?

1. sometimes	7. arrangement	12. sadly
2. something	8. behaviour	13. apparently
3. does	9. immediate	14. acknowledge
4. parents	10. gradually	15. writing
5. unsuccessful	11. college	16. sincerely
6. recent		

Again study the above list of frequently misspelt words, all of which are contained in the following passage. When you have done this ask someone to dictate the passage to you.

PREPARED DICTATION

Geoffrey's parents are sadly disappointed with his recent College report. His mathematics assignments are apparently all too often incorrect and unfinished. Unless he does something quickly about the illogical and inconsistent arrangement of his work, he will certainly be unsuccessful in the coming examinations. The English language tutor is similarly uncomplimentary. Geoffrey's essays are immature and frequently completely irrelevant. Misspellings and grammatical inaccuracies abound and his writing is sometimes totally illegible. Most tutors acknowledge a temporary improvement during February but gradually there has been a steady deterioration since. They criticise his unpredictable behaviour and general impoliteness and it is sincerely hoped there will be an immediate and noticeable improvement.

Suffixes

With most words in our language, we just tack on prefixes and suffixes and that is that. However, there are a few very large groups of words which we have to handle with more care when adding suffixes. I shall deal with these groups in this section.

If ever you have been guilty of writing 'The sun was *shinning* brightly' or 'I did not find her *arguement* convincing' or 'They *payed* too much for their house', then this section is for you.

If you are a good speller but you sometimes hesitate over the number of T's in 'budgeting' or wonder whether 'galloping' should have two P's you will also find this section helpful.

THE ONE–ONE–ONE SPELLING RULE

Look at these words and consider what they have in common:

spot	net	pad	fit
sad	hot	thin	plan
mud	mop	beg	drip

Each word is **one** syllable and ends in **one** consonant preceded by **one** vowel. (Read *Terms You Need to Know* (pages 95–6) if you are not sure what this means.)

A convenient way of referring briefly to such words is to call them 'one–one–one' words.

The following explanation of the rule is concerned with words such as these and what happens to them when suffixes are added.

<table>
<tr>
<td rowspan="2">**Rule 6**</td>
<td>**(a)**</td>
<td>No change to one—one—one word when adding consonant suffix.
Example: hot HOTly</td>
</tr>
<tr>
<td>**(b)**</td>
<td>Double final consonant of one—one—one word when adding vowel suffix.
Example: hot HOTTer</td>
</tr>
</table>

Note: The rule does *not* apply to words like cOOl (two vowels) and daRN (two consonants at end). These words are quite straightforward and suffixes can be added without any basic modification (e.g. COOLing winds, she was DARNing socks). The one—one—one words we are concerned with here, on the other hand, sometimes double their final consonant (SPOTTed) and sometimes do not (SPOTless). Remember these two words or any other pair you happen to know already as a memory key to the one—one—one spelling rule.

EXERCISE 57

Complete the following. All base words are one—one—one words and you can apply the rule safely in every case.

1. lop + ed
2. prim + ly
3. beg + ar
4. scan + ing

5. leg + less
6. sun + y
7. mop + ing

8. wrap + ed
9. fret + ful
10. rim + less

EXERCISE 58

Complete the following. This time try to do so without looking back at the rule. Remember that —Y (as a suffix) counts as a vowel. All words are one—one—one words.

1. prig + ish
2. pit + ed
3. thin + ly
4. fog + y

5. skip + ing
6. big + er
7. dim + ing

8. slip + ed
9. sad + ness
10. run + er

EXERCISE 59

All the words in brackets which follow are also one—one—one words.

Join the base word and suffix (in brackets), doubling the final consonant of the base word when necessary.

1. The Queen was cheered loudly as she (step + ed) out of the car.
2. Don't stand there (chat + ing) when there is work to be done!
3. Don't mention such (sin + ful) thoughts.
4. The prisoner had a (scar + ed) face and (mud + y) boots.
5. We (pat + ed) the poor cat dry.
6. The little breeze barely (stir + ed) the leaves.
7. The butterfly (flit + ed) from one flower to the next.
8. My children love (rub + ing) out mistakes.
9. David is a very (man + ly) little boy.
10. Those holes in the door-frame should be (plug + ed).
11. Their teacher stared thoughtfully at their (grin + ing) faces.
12. Deirdre slowly (sip + ed) her lemonade.
13. We enjoyed (sit + ing) in the sun.
14. My aunt (dip + ed) one toe in the water.

EXERCISE 60

Join the base word and suffix (in brackets), doubling the final consonant of the base word where necessary. Be on your guard. Not all the words here are one–one–one words!

1. The rabbit (hop + ed) inquisitively around the garden.
2. The actress (knit + ed) at rehearsal when she was not (need + ed) on stage.
3. The little boy was (dig + ing) a hole to Australia.
4. My daughter was forever (drop + ing) stitches when she was (learn + ing) to knit.
5. Mrs. Leighton (hug + ed) her daughter when she returned.
6. That is the (big + est) fish I have ever seen.
7. You will need (plan + ing) permission for that extension.
8. Elsie (pin + ed) the pattern carefully to the material.
9. Such films should be (ban + ed).
10. I don't want to be served by waitresses in (top + less) dresses.
11. The boys rushed (mad + ly) down the road.
12. I would prefer a (wood + en) tray.

13. Who is (snap + ing) his fingers?
14. The two (war + ing) countries refused to come to the conference.
15. My grocer (flat + ly) refused to deliver the order.
16. She (tap + ed) her finger nervously.
17. She is the most (snob + ish) person I have ever met.
18. Have you ever (skin + ed) a rabbit?
19. The (dim + ness) was rather depressing.
20. The patient (seem + ed) much better the next day.
21. She (slip + ed) quietly from the (dim + ly)-lit (sit + ing) room.

Special note

Remember that one-syllabled words like 'quit' come within the scope of our rule (we shall have to consider the obligatory U after the Q as part of that consonant, followed by one vowel I and one consonant T).

Thus we have:

QUITTed   QUITTing

Exceptions to the one–one–one rule

There are a few exceptions to this rule but I don't think they will cause you any difficulty. The exceptions are easily summarised. Never double the final consonant if X, W or Y (the word would look so peculiar), so we have sawING, waxED, layING. You can apply the rule safely in every other case, provided the word is one–one–one.

The following spelling lists consist of frequently misspelt words used in the two dictation passages which follow. Read the lists carefully then ask someone to dictate the passages to you. Both passages can be used together if time permits, as they form a continuous narrative.

Can you spell these words?

1. neighbour
2. enthusiastically
3. awkward
4. unusual
5. woollen
6. volunteered

| 7. foreign | 9. assistance | 10. decided |
| 8. niece | | |

1. tedious	5. arrival	8. chocolates
2. interrupted	6. finished	9. annoyed
3. nephew	7. succeeded	10. interesting
4. unreasonably		

PREPARED DICTATION

My foreign neighbour had decided to make her niece a woollen skirt as a surprise birthday present. She was always desperately busy so I volunteered my assistance. She accepted gladly and we enthusiastically planned to start work at eight o'clock. Fitting the loose pattern pieces on the material was quite awkward as the design was an unusual one but we finally managed it.

It was a relief when we had succeeded in pinning everything in position. When the tedious cutting-out was over, we stitched away madly, chatting about our families and any interesting gossip. It was pleasant munching chocolates, sitting side by side at the beautifully polished dining table in that familiar room. We were quite unreasonably annoyed to be interrupted by the arrival of her nephew. The skirt was hemmed, pressed, slipped on a hanger, and hidden. We had completely finished and we grinned happily at each other.

THE SILENT –E RULE

Look carefully at the examples below.

1) She PLANNED her work carefully. (to PLAN)
2) He TAPPED nervously on the door. (to TAP)
3) The little boy HOPPED along the path. (to HOP)

The verbs in the above sentences are all one–one–one words, coming within the scope of Rule 6 which we have just studied.

Such words are often confused with words ending in a silent –E

52

(sometimes called mute −E, or lazy −E or, more excitingly, magic −E). Examples of silent −E words are given in the four sentences below.

4) He PLANED the wood lovingly. (to PLANE)
5) The electrician TAPED the wires. (to TAPE)
6) My grandfather HOPED to come. (to HOPE)
7) He was HOPING to come. (to HOPE)

You never have to double a consonant in a silent −E word. The problem is whether to retain or drop the final −E of the word.

Look at the following words carefully.

spite + ful	spiteFUL	believe + er	believER
sincere + ly	sincereLY	declare + ation	declaraTION
scarce + ly	scarceLY	take + ing	takING
late + ly	lateLY	craze + y	crazY
some + thing	someTHING	define + ition	definITION
safe + ty	safeTY	write + ing	writING

We can formulate the rule as follows:

Rule 7

(a) Keep the −E when adding a consonant suffix to a silent −E word.

Example: like + ly = likeLY

(b) Drop the −E when adding a vowel suffix to a silent −E word.

Example: like + ing = liking

EXERCISE 61

Complete the following. Look back at the rule as often as you wish.

1. love + ly
2. love + ing
3. definite + ly
4. participate + ation
5. late + ly
6. umpire + ing

53

7. prove + ing   9. pav + ed   10. like + ing
8. live + ing

EXERCISE 62

Do the same with the following words.

1. arrange + ment   5. large + ly   8. pine + ing
2. craze + y   6. care + ful   9. achieve + ment
3. like + ly   7. like + able   10. ignore + ance
4. desire + able

EXERCISE 63

Try to complete the words in this exercise without looking back at the rule.

1. severe + ly   5. noise + y   8. some + thing
2. laze + ing   6. define + ing   9. expense + ive
3. lose + ing   7. separate + ly   10. use + ful
4. immense + ly

If you are making mistakes, it is worth learning 'loving' and 'lovely' as a memory key to the rule.

Now revise the rule carefully and complete the following exercise from memory.

EXERCISE 64

1. The three children were (make + ing) a noise.
2. I can see a (define + ite) (improve + ment) in your work.
3. Try (breathe + ing) through your nose!
4. It is quite (like + ly) that they will have to move.
5. It was an (immense + ly) (move + ing) occasion.
6. Sarah was (hope + ing) you would be (come + ing).
7. (Fortunate + ly) the (broke + en) part is not lost.
8. I felt so (lone + ly) when my husband died.
9. The shop assistant's legs were (ache + ing) by lunchtime.

10. Anna's (excite + ment) was intense as the curtain went up.
11. Were you (nerve + ous) dancing in front of so many people?
12. The canvassers (decide + ed) to interview the residents (separate + ly).
13. It is (large + ly) my brother's fault that your car is (damage + ed).
14. The (prepare + ations) were all complete.

EXERCISE 65

Try one more exercise before I deal with the few exceptions there are to Rule 7. Do your very best to get full marks. This is a very important rule that affects thousands of words.

1. He spoke very (sincere + ly).
2. (Give + ing) is easier than (receive + ing).
3. His remarks were (extreme + ly) provocative.
4. Your present will be most (use + ful).
5. Few people are capable of (tame + ing) lions and tigers.
6. The old man's (devote + ion) to his dog was very touching.
7. Try (praise + ing) his efforts (some + times).
8. They are (share + ing) the money between them.

Exceptions

The few exceptions to the rule fall into four categories.

1) The −E is dropped in the following eight words before a consonant suffix:

truly	duly	ninth
argument	wholly	awful
whilst	wisdom	

(Remember: *Truly* and *duly* the *ninth argument* is *wholly awful.*)

2) The −E is retained before a vowel suffix in words like:

gorgeOUS   courageOUS   manageABLE
noticeABLE

(The reason is that before a, o, u, the letters C and G sound hard (e.g. Cat and Got).

The −E after C and G in the words above softens them. G sounds like J in 'courageous'. It is the retention of the letter −E that has made this happen.)

3) The −E is retained in the words below to prevent confusion:

dyeing is different from dying;
singeing is different from singing, etc.

These words look more familiar with −E:

ageing	shoeing	hoeing
mileage	toeing	canoeing
queueing, etc.		

Note: judgement *or* judgment, acknowledgement *or* acknowledgment.

4) A few words ending in −CE change to −CI− before −OUS and −AL, such as:

vice   vicious   race   racial

Note: Learn if you can the eight words listed above in 1. Try to remember the principle behind 2, 3 and 4. However, if in doubt follow the rule and forget the exceptions. It's safer!

EXERCISE 66

In the following exercise, add the suffixes as before to the base words in brackets, but be on your guard for exceptions to the rule.

1. I am (true + ly) sorry for my (late + ness).
2. He very (wise + ly) remained silent.
3. (Fortunate + ly) the (broke + en) part is (replace + able).
4. (Love + ing) one's enemies is not very easy.
5. It is an (outrage + ous) (argue + ment).
6. Autumn is the best time for (prune + ing) roses.
7. (Time + ing) is very important.
8. The two cats were (hope + ing) for an early meal.
9. The (nine + th) box is (complete + ly) empty.
10. The (dine + ing) room is now full.

56

As you will have noticed there may not be many exceptions to Rule 7 but there are some very commonly-used words among them! It really is worth learning these by heart if you can.

BRIEF REVISION EXERCISE BASED ON RULES 6 AND 7

So many spelling errors arise from confusion between one—one—one words and silent —E words that I would like you to have a chance of testing your own grasp of Rules 6 and 7. Read the rules through again if you wish before doing the following exercise from memory by correctly adding the suffix to the base word.

EXERCISE 67

1. We were (hope + ing) the sun would shine.
2. The men (rob + ing) the bank were caught in the act.
3. Try (hop + ing) twenty times up and down the path.
4. They siphoned off the petrol with some plastic (tube + ing).
5. Class 3 will visit the (can + ing) factory next term.
6. The wicked fairy was (bide + ing) her time.
7. The lad was (shin + ing) up the greasy pole.
8. Amelia, you're (slop + ing) the water everywhere!
9. I am glad that (cane + ing) has been abolished.
10. The poor dog is (pine + ing) for his master.
11. Petronella's bedroom had a (slope + ing) ceiling.
12. Henry and Ricky were (plan + ing) their holiday.
13. Mary was (pin + ing) up the hem at the time.
14. Don't stand so close when I am (plane + ing) wood.
15. The sun was (shine + ing) brightly by ten o'clock.

Can you spell these words?

1. approached	5. conscientious	9. twelfth
2. moment	6. typically	10. success
3. opportunity	7. careers	11. period
4. honestly	8. earnest	12. syllabus

Again study the above list of frequently misspelt words before asking someone to dictate the following passage to you. All the words are used in the passage.

PREPARED DICTATION

As the Easter holidays gradually approached, most candidates wisely began revising in earnest. A few of the more conscientious ones carefully divided their revision of the syllabus into the months, weeks and days that remained. Others let the opportunity for planning such sensible schemes slip past. All were sincerely hoping they would somehow be ready when the time came but typically a few honestly admitted to pinning their hopes of success largely on luck and the inspiration of the moment. The results, on which their future careers depended, were due on the twelfth day of August. The period for congratulations and commiserations still lay ahead.

THE –Y RULE EXPANDED

We considered nouns ending in –Y when we were discussing plurals earlier in the book and we noticed then that Rule 3 (see pages 29–33) also applied to infinitives ending in –Y. In discussing the *various* suffixes that can be added to words ending in –Y, we are really expanding this earlier rule.

Look carefully at the two lists below.

delay	delayED, delayING		beauty	beautIFUL
deploy	deployED, deployMENT		mystery	mysterIOUS
pray	prayING, prayER		early	earlIER
play	playING, playER		busy	busINESS
enjoy	enjoyING, enjoyMENT		lonely	lonelINESS
betray	betrayING, betrayAL		deny	denIED

Once again, you will see, you have to distinguish between words ending in a **vowel** + Y and a **consonant** + Y. You *must* know the difference between a vowel and a consonant. (If in doubt refer to *Terms You Need to Know* on pages 95–6.)

<table>
<tr>
<td rowspan="2">**Rule 8**</td>
<td>**(a)** If there is a vowel before the −**Y**, just add suffix.

Example: enjoy enjoyED</td>
</tr>
<tr>
<td>**(b)** If there is a consonant before the −**Y**, change the Y to an I when you add suffix (unless suffix begins with I. You don't want two I's together).

Examples: try trIED (but trYing)
cry crIED (but crYing)</td>
</tr>
</table>

There are a few exceptions which will be given in a moment but first try some exercises based on adding vowel and consonant suffixes to regular words.

Remember this rule follows exactly the same pattern as the rule for the plural or words ending in Y. Just as 'boy' became 'boys', so now 'betray' becomes 'betrayED' or 'betrayING'.

EXERCISE 68

Look carefully at the following examples. Why does the Y change to I in every case?

1. beauty + ful
2. apply + ance
3. try + ed
4. early + er
5. empty + ed
6. busy + ly
7. ally + ed
8. deny + ed
9. pry + ed
10. try + al

Remember it makes no difference whether the *suffix* is a vowel or a consonant one. The vital factor is the ending of the base word.

EXERCISE 69

Look carefully at these examples. Why is there no change to the Y of the base word when a suffix is added? Remember there are two possible reasons.

1. delay + ed
2. pray + ing
3. satisfy + ing
4. enjoy + ed
5. fly + ing
6. study + ing
7. slay + ing
8. bray + ed
9. try + ing
10. pry + ing

EXERCISE 70

In this exercise join the suffix to the base word, changing Y to I where necessary. Try not to look back at the rule.

1. reply + ed
2. reply + ing
3. deny + al
4. deny + ed
5. plenty + ful
6. destroy + er
7. play + ed
8. supply + er
9. supply + ing
10. petrify + ed

As you will have found, it is necessary to be very vigilant! However, it is much easier to learn a rule that applies to hundreds and thousands of words than it is to learn each of those words individually. Remember *frayed* but *fried* as a memory key.

EXERCISE 71

Complete the following.

1. penny + less
2. putrefy + ing
3. ply + ed
4. jockey + ing
5. portray + ing
6. mystify + ed
7. survey + or
8. relay + ing
9. prey + ing
10. forty + eth

Exceptions

We come now to the exceptions. These you will have to learn individually. I have put an asterisk beside the words you are likely to want most frequently. If in doubt, follow the rule and forget the exceptions but learn the exceptions if you can. The exceptions are:

* 1. laid (mislaid, etc)
* 2. paid (repaid, etc)
* 3. said
  4. slain
* 5. daily
  6. gaily
  7. gaiety
  8. ski-ing
  9. taxi-ing
  10. shyly, shyer, shyest
  11. slyly, slyer, slyest
  12. wryly
  13. babyhood
  14. dryness

Possibly skiing and taxiing are the only words in the English language where two I's appear together and then we sometimes separate them a little by using a hyphen.

EXERCISE 72

Complete the following words. Beware some exceptions to the rule.

1. day + ly
2. pay + ed
3. defy + ance
4. betray + al
5. study + ous
6. happy + ness
7. lonely + ness
8. lay + ed
9. copy + ed
10. modify + ed

EXERCISE 73

Try again with this exercise. Again beware of exceptions.

1. carry + age
2. mercy + ful
3. enjoy + ment
4. say + ed
5. heavy + ly
6. busy + ness
7. glory + ous
8. fly + ing
9. lazy + est
10. gay + ly

EXERCISE 74

Revise the rule and exceptions and then try to complete the words in this exercise from memory.

1. The children were seen (hurry + ing) down the road.
2. I shall never forget her (lovely + ness) that evening.
3. Stephen packed his case in (ready + ness) for the journey.
4. The Chairman apologised for having (mislay + ed) his book.
5. The clergyman (pity + ed) the poor soul with all his heart.
6. I (envy + ed) her willingness and energy!
7. I was sure John had (copy + ed) Robert's work.
8. (Day + ly) she lit the fire at 6.0 a.m.
9. There was a (dry + ness) in Mrs. Norman's throat as she thanked the girls for the last time.
10. Her husband (try + ed) to erect the tent by himself but failed dismally.
11. The unknown knight (parry + ed) all his blows (easy + ly).
12. Who (supply + ed) the tools?
13. They (say + ed) they were not coming.

Can you spell these words?

1. reference
2. reassurance
3. supposed
4. routine
5. loneliness
6. pensioner
7. immensely
8. information
9. librarian
10. recommend

Study the word list above, which again consists of frequently mis-spelt words, all of which are used in the following passage, then get someone to dictate the passage to you.

DICTATION

Sheila Brown was a trainee librarian. She discovered that she enjoyed the work immensely and would recommend librarianship enthusiasti-cally as a career. It was enjoyable meeting the public and trying to help those who needed assistance. She noticed some pensioners came daily to the Reference Library. They read periodicals steadily all morning. She supposed the routine was a reassurance to them and eased the loneliness of retirement a little. After school and college each day, students filled the Reference Room, copying information studiously from encyclopaedias. She was busiest of all on Saturdays when whole families changed their books.

TWO–ONE–ONE RULE

This rule applies to words of **two** syllables which have **one** final consonant preceded by **one** vowel. So far it may sound rather like Rule 6 (one–one–one) (pages 48–52) but at this point any similarity ends.

It is a useful rule (which many people are regularly grateful for) but it is difficult to grasp at first.

Consider the following:

gallop   he gallopS   they gallopED
begin   she beginS   you are beginnING

Both 'gallop' and 'begin' are two–one–one words; both base words remain unchanged when the consonant S is added; 'gallop' remains unchanged as a base word when the vowel suffix ED is added, 'begin' doubles its final letter before the vowel suffix ING. Why?

It is not so arbitrary as it looks! In fact, it is how the word *sounds* rather than how it looks that is important.

There is an important difference between the stress in the word 'gallop' and the stress in the word 'begin'. If you exaggerate the stress, you will see you emphasise the first syllable in one (GALlop) and the second syllable in the other (beGIN).

Rule 9

(a) There is *no* change to a two—one—one base word when a **consonant** suffix is added.

Examples: allotMENT   forgetFUL
numberLESS   tenderNESS

(b) Take care when adding a **vowel** suffix. If stress on first syllable, have **one** consonant before adding suffix.

Examples: ORbit   orbiTed   orbiTing
FASTen   fasteNed   fasteNing

If stress on second syllable, have **two** final consonants before adding suffix.

Examples: occur   occuRRed
subMIT   submiTTed

Clearly the successful application of this rule will depend on the ability of the student to determine which syllable of a two-syllabled word is stressed.

It may be helpful to incorporate the word in a sentence and then to try stressing first one syllable and then the other.

If your ear does not help you, your dictionary will. The main accent will be shown by this mark ´ which will usually be placed *after* the stressed syllable. Thus GALlop is shown as gall´op and beGIN as begin´.

Don't be confused by the different symbols positioned over the vowels; these help with pronunciation not stress.

Read the following ten words aloud to yourself. Exaggerate the stress. Can you see that the stress is on the first syllable of each word? (In other words, you say it more heavily.)

pivot	market	offer
alter	hamper	gallop
number	orbit	budget
lengthen		

In the following words, the stress is on the second syllable. Read them aloud, exaggerating the stress, so that you are quite clear what is meant.

forbid	permit (verb)	compel
outwit	recur	outbid
regret	begin	admit
propel		

Notice the *verb* 'permit' is 'permit' with the stress on the second syllable. The *noun* 'permit' has the stress on the first syllable. There are other words like this.

Decide where the stress comes in the following words.

EXERCISE 75

1. omit	8. label	15. appal
2. limit	9. prefer	16. quarrel
3. impel	10. fasten	17. patrol
4. differ	11. transmit	18. profit
5. occur	12. worship	19. debar
6. hasten	13. submit	20. packet
7. commit	14. travel	

In the above exercise, the even numbers have the stress on the first syllable and the odd numbers have the stress on the second. If you want more practice, try the following exercise.

EXERCISE 76

Decide where the stress comes.

1. hinder	8. annul	15. peter (*v*)
2. acquit	9. cancel	16. prefer
3. enter	10. defer	17. pedal
4. equip	11. signal	18. repel
5. happen	12. infer	19. ballot (*v*)
6. excel	13. rivet	20. allot
7. suffer	14. expel	

Here the even numbers have the stress on the second syllable and it is the odd numbers that have the stress on the first.

Make sure you understand what is meant by stressing the first or the second syllable before applying Rule 9 to the following exercises.

EXERCISE 77

Complete the following.

1. limit + ing	5. admit + ing	8. equip + ment
2. profit + able	6. alter + ation	9. forbid + en
3. worship + ful	7. equip + ing	10. market + ing
4. commit + al		

Don't worry if you are making mistakes at this stage. Look again at the rule and try the following exercises.

EXERCISE 78

Complete the following.

1. begin + ing	3. forget + ing	5. limit + less
2. allot + ment	4. forget + ful	6. omit + ing

7. listen + ing   9. acquit + ed   10. regret + ed
8. gossip + ed

EXERCISE 79

Add suffixes to the two−one−one base words as indicated.

1. Am I (permit + ed) to smoke?
2. They enjoy (garden + ing) and (potter + ing).
3. The enterprise was a (profit + able) one.
4. The Prince of Wales (pilot + ed) the 'plane.
5. I am afraid your days as Chairman are (number + ed).
6. Your aunt has bought you a (digit + al) watch.
7. The little boy (outwit + ed) both parents.
8. The astronauts have (orbit + ed) Venus.
9. (Packet + ed) biscuits always cost more.
10. My husband (order + ed) me to wash up.
11. The house will be quieter when the rooms are (carpet + ed).
12. The neighbours have been (gossip + ing) again.
13. Nathan (submit + ed) reluctantly to a dental inspection.
14. The programme on badgers will be (transmit + ed) at the week-end.
15. The boulder was (lever + ed) into position.
16. After a few yards the path (peter + ed) out.
17. You were (hammer + ing) into the early hours.
18. You should make allowances. He is a (begin + er).
19. Those accounts must be (audit + ed).

NOTE: There is *change of stress* in the following words and so sometimes the final consonant of the base word is doubled, sometimes it is not.

conFER	conFERRed	conFERRing	CONference
deFER	deFERRed	deFERRing	DEFerence
preFER	preFERRed	preFERRing	PREFerence
reFER	reFERRed	reFERRing	REFerence
transFER	transFERRed	transFERRing	TRANSference

Exceptions

There are some exceptions and these are listed below.

1) All two–one–one words ending in –L are a special case and are dealt with below.

2) WORSHIP, KIDNAP, HANDICAP (actually three syllables but included here) and OUTFIT always double final consonant before a vowel suffix despite stress on first syllable, so we have worshippED, outfittER, etc.

3) Words ending in –W, –X and –Y never double despite stress because they would look so odd, so betrayED, relaxED, allowED.

L is a special case

Two–one–one words ending in –L follow a modified version of Rule 9.

1) As with Rule 9 earlier, there is no change to base word when a consonant suffix is added.

   (e.g. quarrel + some = quarrelsome
         annul + ment = annulment)

2) When using a vowel suffix, unlike Rule 9 earlier, ignore whether stress is on the first or second syllable, *double* the L before the suffix.

   (e.g. quarrel + ed = quarrelled annul + ing = annulling)

Exceptions

1) parallel parallelED   parallelOGRAM

2) Never double before –ITY.

   (e.g. formalITY   civilITY)

3) Never double before –ISE or –IZE.

   (e.g. legal legalISE   penal penalISE)

EXERCISE 80

Join base words and suffixes. Note all base words here end in L.

1. We shall pay by (instal + ments).
             (install + ments). (Alternative spelling.)
2. (Excel + ent)!
3. I very much regret the (cancel + ation).
4. Would you enjoy (label + ing) bottles all your life?
5. The little boy was (pedal + ing) furiously.
6. What an (appal + ing) tragedy!
7. He has always been a (quarrel + some) child.

EXERCISE 81

Treat the following as a revision exercise of the two—one—one rule and its exceptions. Look again at the rule if you wish *before* doing the exercise.

1. They were both (debar + ed) from membership.
2. The authorities were (compel + ed) to give way.
3. The chairman (omit + ed) all mention of the committee.
4. I think your marriage could be (annul + ed) in the circumstances.
5. I was (rivet + ed) by the book.
6. The crowd was bitterly disappointed at the (cancel + ation) of the match.
7. We (signal + ed) to the waiting man.
8. Couldn't production of the chemical be (limit + ed)?
9. The huntsman (gallop + ed) briskly away.
10. The worried woman had not (budget + ed) for such an expense.
11. Joe Green (admit + ed) he was responsible.
12. The members will have to be (ballot + ed) before a decision is reached.
13. The Scarlet Pimpernel (outwit + ed) them all.
14. (Pivot + ing) on one foot, the ballerina smiled bravely.
15. It is a (recur + ent) problem.
16. He (prefer + ed) to go alone.
17. We (follow + ed) the little lane until it (peter + ed) out.
18. The doctor advised her to reduce her (commit + ments).

19. All the family are hoping for an (acquit + al).
20. Your father has (forbid + en) you to wear that dress.
21. (Inter + ment) will be at 3.00 p.m. Family mourners only, please.
22. We have a very small garden and hope to get an (allot + ment) if the waiting list is not too long.

Two short exercises follow for those who need additional practice. Remember you can check your work by reference to the check list on pages 88–94.

EXERCISE 82

Join base word and suffix.

1. profit + able
2. occur + ence
3. equip + ed
4. equip + ment
5. budget + ed
6. profit + ed
7. outwit + ing
8. propel + er
9. offer + ed
10. travel + er

EXERCISE 83

Join base word and suffix.

1. fasten + ing
2. regret + ful
3. forbid + en
4. market + able
5. repel + ed
6. patrol + ed
7. worship + ing
8. omit + ed
9. begin + er
10. hamper + ing

Can you spell these words?

1. opinion
2. viewed
3. mortgage
4. colossal
5. decision
6. believe
7. character
8. choice
9. attitude
10. autumn
11. Christmas
12. buildings

As before, carefully study this word list before asking someone to dictate the following passage to you. The passage contains all these words, which are frequently misspelt.

PREPARED DICTATION

We were searching for reasonably-priced accommodation in the village and in our opinion we had a severely limited choice. We tried to ignore the appalling decorative state of some of the buildings we viewed but we discovered that nicely-carpeted floors and prettily-papered walls did have an effect on our attitude. Finally we bought a thatched cottage which had been pitifully neglected. We enjoyed restoring it to its former character. We hammered, we chiselled, we plastered, we levelled. We laboured all that autumn and by Christmas we were beginning to believe it would never be finished. However, nobody regretted the decision to buy, despite the colossal mortgage.

REVISION TEST

A revision test consisting of eight exercises on the four rules dealt with in this section now follows. When you have completed the exercises check your work by reference to the check list appearing on pages 88–94; analyse your mistakes carefully and look again very closely at the rules you have not fully grasped. Marks are out of one hundred.

EXERCISE 84

Join base word and suffix.

1. pedal + ing
2. slope + ing
3. bathe + ing
4. begin + ing
5. refer + ing
6. exchange + able
7. loose + ness
8. lone + ly
9. net + ed
10. mercy + ful

EXERCISE 85

Do the same again.

1. canoe + ing
2. pin + ing
3. skip + ed
4. rot + en
5. beauty + ful
6. prefer + ed
7. spoil + ing
8. try + ed
9. ski + ing
10. pivot + ing

EXERCISE 86

Complete the following.

1. The (dry + ness) of the soil was surprising.
2. The elderly often experience great (lonely + ness).
3. Why not check your facts in the (Refer + ence) Library?
4. I did not expect such (formal + ity).
5. The astronauts were (orbit + ing) the earth while we slept.
6. This is one of the (hot + est) days this year.
7. We all admired the exquisite flower (arrange + ment).
8. Trevor arrived at (approximate + ly) 10.30 a.m.
9. Mrs. Green feels that her son is already (benefit + ing) from the treatment.
10. Deborah will not be (come + ing) now.

EXERCISE 87

Join base word and suffix.

1. live + ing
2. submit + ing
3. early + er
4. essay + ist
5. notice + ing
6. gallop + ed
7. forget + ful
8. enjoy + ed
9. wage + ed
10. compel + ing

EXERCISE 88

Complete as above.

1. argue + ment
2. squeeze + ing
3. wage + ing
4. hug + ing
5. true + ly
6. scrape + ing
7. hurry + ed
8. achieve + ment
9. busy + ness
10. drop + let

EXERCISE 89

Add suffix to base word as before.

1. Bob's handwriting is quite (differ + ent) from Alan's.
2. The cadets now have all the (equip + ment) they need.

71

3. Painting the ceiling black was (definite + ly) a mistake.
4. It was an (excite + ing) moment for us all.
5. I am sure that you will be (pay + ed).
6. I was (frighten + ed) by his tone.
7. (Move + ing) into a house of her own was the (fulfil + ment) of the dream of a life-time.
8. The Fire Brigade came (immediate + ly).
9. Your (ignore + ance) of the social graces is (unforgive + able).
10. I will trust your (judge + ment).
11. We have not seen you (late + ly).
12. It is not (like + ly) that they will lose their (lively + hood).
13. What a delicious apple-tart! You are a (marvel + ous) cook.
14. The small boy blew his nose (noisy + ly).
15. The accident (occur + ed) just after mid-night.
16. Is he a (qualify + ed) solicitor?
17. We have (profit + ed) from our experience.

EXERCISE 90

Complete the following.

1. air + less
2. quarrel + ing
3. ballot + ed
4. deny + al
5. appeal + ing
6. lobby + ist
7. big + er
8. chirrup + ing
9. true + ly
10. steam + er
11. crib + age
12. advantage + ous
13. repel + ed
14. shy + ness
15. rivet + ing
16. sandal + ed
17. age + ing
18. fit + ness
19. recur + ence
20. imperil + ed

EXERCISE 91

Add –ED to these verbs, making any necessary changes to the base word.

1. He (lop) the branches.
2. The housewives (shop) in London.
3. The dog (pine) for his master.
4. We were (wine) and (dine) at Claridges.

5. I (hope) you would come.
6. The flag seller (pin) the poppy in his lapel.
7. Are all the jam jars (label) now?
8. The cargo will be (ship) to South Africa.
9. The two girls (ignore) the boys' comments.

Total your marks for this test out of one hundred. It will be a good indication of how firm your grasp of the four rules within this section is. You *must* know Rules 6, 7 and 8. Rule 9 is more difficult to understand and difficult for students to grasp, particularly for those working on their own.

Additional Aids

This section deals first with the IE, EI rule. Students are often heard quoting 'I before E except after C' and then discovering that there are so many exceptions to the rule that it is not much help.

It is well worth learning the *complete* jingle below. There are, in fact, a total of twenty-two exceptions (see pages 75–6) and it *is* possible to learn these by heart. If you make the necessary effort to do this, you need never make a mistake with this group of words again.

IE, EI WORDS

Rule 10	Spell such words **IE** in most cases (e.g. niece, friend, pier).
	Spell them **EI**:
	1) If the two vowels come immediately after C (e.g. deceive, receipt, ceiling). There are eight exceptions given on pages 75–6.
	2) If the two vowels rhyme with A (e.g. veil, freight, reindeer) or AIR (e.g. heir, their).
	3) If included in list of fourteen exceptions given on page 75.
	The jingle that sums up most of this very neatly is this:
	I before E except after C *or when sounded like A as in neighbour and weigh.*

In Exercises 92 and 93 apply Rule 10 to the sentences: remember it is always IE unless there is a good reason why it should be EI.

EXERCISE 92

1. She held the r__ns lightly.
2. There are __ght spare places on the coach.
3. My nephew is so conc__ted.
4. I doubt if she would d__gn to notice us.
5. Everyone must dress as a Caval__r or a Roundhead.
6. P__rce the top to let the air out.
7. I rec__ved your letter on Friday.
8. Do you know th__r address?
9. We are going to buy a golden retr__ver.
10. Prince Charles is h__r to the throne.

EXERCISE 93

Try again with this exercise.

1. perc__ve
2. sk__n
3. dec__t
4. h__r
5. th__r
6. f__ld
7. gr__ve
8. br__f
9. conc__ve
10. d__gn

Exceptions

We come now to the 22 exceptions followed by five more exercises based on IE/EI words. By the time you have worked through them carefully you may well have memorised the exceptions!

EI **not** after C (14 exceptions)

either	neither	counterfeit	foreign
forfeit	heifer	height	leisure
protein	seize	sovereign	surfeit
weir	weird		

Plus some Christian names (Keith, Neil, Sheila, Deirdre, etc.).

IE **after** C (8 exceptions)

ancient	conscience	deficient	efficient

proficient   sufficient   species   glacier
(All except last pronounced 'sh'.)

Note: heinous pronounced 'a' therefore regular.

EXERCISE 94

Insert IE or EI. Be on your guard. Exceptions are included.

1. anc__nt
2. n__ghbour
3. p__rce
4. gr__vance
5. __ther
6. defic__nt
7. rec__pt
8. for__gner
9. gr__f
10. n__ce

EXERCISE 95

Do the same here. Beware exceptions.

1. n__ther
2. spec__s
3. counterf__t
4. l__sure
5. f__nd
6. w__rd
7. c__ling
8. effic__nt
9. surf__t
10. h__ght
11. s__ze
12. m__n
13. profic__nt
14. retr__ve
15. bel__f
16. consc__nce
17. prot__n
18. h__nous
19. glac__r
20. w__r

EXERCISE 96

Revise the rule again and look through the exceptions. See if you can do the following exercise without looking back.

1. My n__ce will be __ghteen tomorrow.
2. The pr__st spoke seriously to Sh__la.
3. A p__rcing shr__k terrified the aud__nce.
4. My n__ghbour bel__ves the world is flat.
5. Our sover__gn, Queen Elizabeth, has r__gned for over twenty-five years.
6. __ght r__ndeer pulled the sl__gh.
7. I was very rel__ved when the th__f was caught.
8. Mr. Charles was delighted to rec__ve your letter.

9. Sandra is having a four t__red wedding cake.
10. Sandringham House has won the Hockey sh__ld.
11. Your ach__vement is remarkable for a boy of your age.
12. In the old days, the tribal ch__ftain w__lded considerable power.
13. The h__fer was sent to market last Tuesday.
14. The head girl was very conc__ted.
15. Her effic__ncy was never called into question.
16. Th__r dog is a black retr__ver.
17. Remember to s__ve the flour.
18. Wisely, the ambushed sold__r f__gned death.

Two more exercises follow for those who would like additional practice. Remember you can check your work by referring to the check list on pages 88–94.

EXERCISE 97

Insert IE or EI.

1. r__ndeer	6. fr__ze	11. r__gn
2. retr__ve	7. effic__nt	12. y__ld
3. consc__nce	8. h__ght	13. for__gn
4. chandel__r	9. th__r	14. w__ght
5. __ghty	10. v__n	15. n__ther

EXERCISE 98

Insert either IE or EI.

1. n__ghbour	6. h__rloom	11. n__gh
2. conc__t	7. forf__t	12. p__ce
3. b__ge	8. fr__ght	13. sh__ld
4. perc__ve	9 h__ress	14. sl__gh
5. h__fer	10. ch__f	15. conc__t

Can you spell these words?

1. Russian	4. regrettable	7. canoeing
2. interests	5. scarcely	8. literature
3. favourite	6. talents	9. accustomed

10. languages	13. different	15. symphony
11. probably	14. priorities	16. occasionally
12. photography		

Before asking someone to dictate the following passage to you, study the list of words which are frequently misspelt. They are all used in the passage.

PREPARED DICTATION

I received a brief but interesting letter from my favourite niece, Deirdre, the day before yesterday. I believe she and her friend are probably studying eight different foreign languages between them. They are naturally gifted but neither young woman is conceited or boasts about her talents. Now that their diploma course is becoming more specialised, they have scarcely any leisure time to themselves. This is really regrettable because each has had to sacrifice worthwhile hobbies and interests. They both enjoy canoeing, photography and Russian literature and are accustomed to going occasionally to a symphony concert. Their studies must come first. They have their priorities right.

THREE SPELLING TIPS

Now that the ten great spelling rules have been dealt with, readers will find the following three spelling tips extremely useful.

Tip one: the suffix −FUL

Note that when FULL is added to a word, it always becomes fuL.

Examples:

| beautifuL | awfuL | hopefuL |
| plentifuL | resourcefuL | pitifuL |

EXERCISE 99

Complete the following by joining base word to suffix (Rule 8 (see pages 58−62) may also be useful).

1. remorse + full	8. fruit + full	15. wist + full
2. wonder + full	9. grate + full	16. grace + full
3. hate + full	10. boast + full	17. master + full
4. mercy + full	11. spite + full	18. fancy + full
5. colour + full	12. peace + full	19. rest + full
6. sorrow + full	13. delight + full	20. dread + full
7. fit + full	14. faith + full	

Tip two: −CAL, −CLE

These two endings sound very similar and it is easy to misspell words as a result of this. It is possible to make a very neat division between the two endings because adjectives (describing words) end in −CAL and nouns (names of objects etc.) end in −CLE.

−CAL (adjectives)	*−CLE (nouns)*
nautical	article
tropical	circle
magical	particle
musical	vehicle
physical	cuticle
clerical	cubicle
logical	bicycle
critical	obstacle
ethical	miracle
theatrical	spectacle
practical, etc.	uncle, etc.

Note: The same principle(!) applies to the words 'principal' and 'principle'. PrinciPAL is the adjective and princiPLE the noun. Remember, though, that the Principal of a College is the PrinciPAL lecturer and therefore we use the adjective form. These two words are included in the following exercise because they cause so much confusion.

EXERCISE 100

Add −AL or −LE to the following.

1. Joan bought an exquisite music__ box in Slough.

79

2. The weight-lifter's physic__ strength was astonishing.
3. I object to the proposal on princip__.
4. Sharon enjoys cleric__ work.
5. The spectac__ of my unc__ on a skateboard was alarming.
6. You can change in a cubic__ at the swimming baths.
7. Fishing nets and floats helped to give a nautic__ atmosphere at the Sub-Aqua Club dance.
8. The only obstac__ to your promotion is your unwillingness to move from the area.
9. We were all very critic__ of the production.
10. A partic__ of metal was lodged in his eye.
11. The Princip__ told all the students that the examinations would be postponed.
12. The little boy was given a tricyc__ for his birthday.
13. Sub-tropic__ plants need careful attention.
14. He gave a demoniac__ laugh.
15. My aunt enjoys historic__ novels.
16. My husband has a rather puritanic__ outlook.
17. It was a mirac__ that no one was hurt.
18. A visit to the Botanic__ Gardens would be very interesting.
19. My sister gave an hysteric__ laugh.

Tip three: extra K

Read these two words aloud: icing, panicking. You will notice that 'icing' is pronounced with an 's' sound in the middle, 'panicking' with a 'k' sound. It is the presence of the 'k' in 'panicking' that keeps the 'c' hard before the 'i' of 'ing'.

There are six words that require the insertion of a 'k' before an 'e', 'i' or 'y' in order to keep the 'c' hard:

panic	mimic	traffic
frolic	bivouac	picnic

Look carefully at the following table:

	K necessary before *e, i, y*	*No K necessary before* *consonants*
panic	panicKed panicKing panicKy	panics panic-monger
traffic	trafficKed trafficKer trafficKing	traffics traffic-less
mimic	mimicKed mimicKing	mimics mimicry
frolic	frolicKed frolicKing	frolics frolicsome
bivouac	bivouacKed bivouacKing	bivouacs
picnic	picnicKed picnicKing picnicKer	picnics

Can you spell these words?

1. fifteen
2. experience
3. liaison
4. famous
5. vehicle
6. unconscious
7. routine
8. neighbouring
9. women
10. resourceful

DICTATION

Fifteen thankful but frightened picnickers were rescued this afternoon from a famous beauty spot on one of the principal mountain passes in Switzerland. They had the frightful experience of seeing a powerful vehicle, quite out of control, careering towards them. The disgraceful driver panicked completely but fortunately a resourceful passenger snatched the steering wheel and managed to brake at the last moment. It was a miracle that no one was fatally injured. The liaison between the emergency services was most impressive and rescue vehicles arrived promptly. All concerned, including two unconscious women, were taken to a neighbouring hospital for routine medical examination.

Can You Spell These Words?

There now follows in alphabetical order a list of all the spellings I have suggested during the course of the book that you should learn by heart. Any other words you got wrong in the dictation passages should be added to this list.

abroad
accommodation
accustomed
acknowledge
across
addressed
advisers
already
among
annoyed
annual
apology
apparently
approached
arrangement
arrival
assistance
attitude
autumn
awkward

beautifully
because
before
behaviour
behind
believe
Britain
building
busily

business

canoeing
careers
certain
character
chocolates
choice
Christmas
clothes
college
colossal
coming
concert
conscientious
could've

decided
decision
definite
different
disappointing
does

earnest
embarrassing
emergency
enthusiastically
excited
exercised

exhausted
experience
extraordinary
extremely

families
famous
favourite
February
fifteen
finally
finished
foreign
forty
frightened
front

ghastly
government
gradually

heard
holiday
honestly

immediate
immensely
information
intentions
interesting

interests	people	success
interrupted	period	suggestion
island	photography	supposed
	pleasant	surprise
language	preferred	surprised
librarian	pretty	syllabus
limit	priorities	symphony
liaison	probably	
literature		talents
loneliness	quality	tedious
lose	quarrelled	thoroughly
luxury	quiet	tired
		tried
mattress	really	truly
meant	reassurance	Tuesday
memories	received	twelfth
Mediterranean	recent	typically
mischievous	recognising	
moment	recommend	unconscious
mortgage	reference	unreasonably
	regrettable	until
necessary	repairing	unsuccessful
neighbour	resourceful	unusual
neighbouring	restaurant	
nephew	routine	valuable
niece	Russian	vehicle
ninety		viewed
	sadly	voiced
occasion	Saturday	volunteered
occasional	scarcely	
occasionally	separate	Wednesday
opinion	severely	whether
opportunity	shining	women
	similar	wondered
parents	sincerely	wondering
Parliament	something	woollen
patience	sometimes	writing
pensioner	succeeded	

Answers to Exercises in Section One

Exercise 1

1. to, to	2. too, to
3. to	4. to
5. too	6. two, too
7. to	8. to

Exercise 2

1. too	2. too, to
3. too, to	4. two
5. to, to	6. too
7. two, to	8. too
9. too	10. to, too
11. to	12. to
13. to	14. too, to

Exercise 3

1. too	2. too, to
3. to	4. to
5. too	6. to
7. too	8. too, to

Exercise 4

1. to	2. to
3. too	4. two
5. too	6. two
7. to	8. too
9. to	10. to

Exercise 5

1. they're	2. there
3. there	4. they're
5. there	6. they're
7. their	8. they're
9. there	10. there

Exercise 6

1. there	2. their
3. there	4. there
5. their	6. there
7. there	8. their
9. their	10. they're

Exercise 7

1. they're	2. their
3. their	4. there
5. there	6. their
7. their	8. there
9. they're	10. there

Exercise 8

1. they're	2. their
3. they're	4. there
5. there	6. their
7. they're	8. their
9. there	10. their

Exercise 9

1. passed	2. past
3. past	4. past
5. past	6. passed
7. past	8. past
9. passed	10. past

Exercise 10

1. past	2. past
3. passed	4. passed
5. past	6. passed
7. passed	8. past
9. passed	10. past

Exercise 11

1. passed	2. past
3. past	4. past
5. passed	6. past
7. past	8. passed
9. passed	10. passed

Exercise 12

1. past	2. passed
3. passed	4. past
5. past	6. past
7. past	8. passed
9. past	10. passed

Exercise 13

1. it's	2. its
3. its	4. its
5. it's	6. it's
7. it's	8. its
9. its	10. its

Exercise 14

1. its	2. it's
3. its	4. it's
5. its	6. its
7. it's	8. it's
9. its	10. it's

Exercise 15

1. where	2. where
3. were	4. were
5. where	6. were
7. where	8. were
9. were	10. where

Exercise 16

1. where	2. were
3. where	4. where
5. were	6. were
7. where	8. where
9. where	10. were

Exercise 17

1. where	2. where
3. where	4. were
5. were	6. were, where
7. were	8. where
9. were, where	10. were
11. were	12. where, were

Exercise 18

1. where	2. where
3. were	4. where
5. where, were	6. where
7. were	8. were
9. were	

Exercise 19

1. lose	2. loose
3. loose	4. lose
5. loose	6. loose
7. loose	8. lose
9. loose	10. loose

Exercise 20

1. loose	2. loose
3. loose	4. lose
5. lose	6. loose
7. lose	8. lose
9. loose	10. lose

Exercise 21

1. effect	2. affect
3. effect	4. effect
5. affect	6. affect
7. effect	8. affect
9. effect	10. effect

Exercise 22

1. affect	2. effect
3. affect, affect	4. affect
5. effect	6. effect
7. affect	8. effect
9. affect	10. effect

Exercise 23

1. practise	2. licence
3. license	4. practice
5. advise	6. prophecy
7. prophesy	8. advice
9. devise	10. practice

Exercise 24

1. practice	2. practise
3. practise	4. practice
5. practice	6. practice
7. practice	8. practise
9. practice	10. practise

Exercise 25

1. licence	2. licence
3. license	4. licence
5. licence	6. licence
7. licence	8. licence
9. license	10. licence

Answers to Revision Tests

Exercise 26

1. too	2. too, to
3. their	4. they're
5. too	6. there
7. to	8. two
9. there	

Exercise 27

1. too	2. too, to
3. too	4. passed
5. there	6. their
7. they're	8. to
9. there	

Exercise 28

1. passed	2. to
3. too	4. past
5. to	6. they're
7. passed	8. there
9. passed	10. past

Exercise 29

1. it's, too, to, to
2. it's, they're
3. they're
4. it's
5. passed
6. it's, too
7. its
8. its
9. their
10. passed

Exercise 30

1. too	2. past
3. were	4. their
5. where	6. to, lose
7. were	8. loose
9. lose	

Exercise 31

1. to	2. to
3. too, to	4. two
5. to	6. to
7. too	8. too/two
9. to	

Exercise 32

1. affect	2. effect
3. effect	4. effect
5. effect	6. affect
7. effect	8. effect
9. affect	10. affect

Exercise 33

1. practise	2. too
3. too	4. they're, to
5. past, it's, too	6. where
7. licence	

Exercise 34

1. clothes	2. of
3. quite	4. to, buy, their
5. knew	6. seem
7. quite, sure	8. who's
9. you're	10. your, through
11. know	

Alphabetical Check List for Exercises 35–100

Check your answers to the exercises in Sections 2–5 by referring to this list.

abbeys
abscesses
achievement
aching
acquittal
acquitted
activities
admitted
admitting
advantageous
advice
advises
ageing
aground
airless
albinos
alleys (s. alley)
allied
allies (s. ally)
allotment
alloys
aloud
alteration
although
always
ancient
annoys
annulled

appalling
appealing
appliance
applies
approximately
argument
arrangement
attorneys
audience
audited
avert
avocados
awful

babies
babyhood
bailiffs
balconies
balloted
banjos
banned
bathing
batteries
beautiful
beggar
beginner
beginning

beige
belief
believes
benches
benefiting
berate
betrayal
biding
bigger
biggest
biros
boastful
botanical
boxes
brayed
brays
breathing
brief
broken
budgeted
buffaloes
bullies
buses
bushes
busily
business
butterflies
buys

cafés
calves
cameos
cancellation
candied
caning (*from* cane)
canning (*from* can)
canoeing
carafes
careful
cargoes
carpeted
carriage
carries
casinos
cavalier
cavies
cast-offs
ceiling
cellos
centuries
chandelier
chapels
chatting
chief
chiefs
chieftain
chirruping
choruses
Christmases
churches
cities
clerical
cliffs
clocks
coaxes
colourful
coming
commandos
committal
commitments
compelled
compelling
completely

conceit
conceited
conceive
conductors
conscience
contraltos
copied
counterfeit
countries
crazy
cribbage
cries
critical
crutches
cuckoos
cubicle
curios

daily
damaged
debarred
deceit
decided
defiance
deficient
defining
definite
definitely
deign
delayed
delays
delightful
demoniacal
denial
denied
denies
depresses
desirable
destroyer
devise
devotion
different
digging
digital

dimly
dimming
dimness
dined
dining
dipped
disable
disability
disagree
disappear
disappointed
disarrange
discredit
dishes
dishevelled
displease
displeased
dissimilar
dominoes
dreadful
dreams
droplet
dropping
dryness
duties
dwarfs
dyeing

earlier
easily
echoes
eccentricities
ecstasies
eddies
efficiency
efficient
eight
eighteen
eighty
either
elves
embellishes
embryos
emissaries

employs	foggy	halves
empresses	foodstuffs	hammering
emptied	followed	hampering
enemies	forbidden	handkerchiefs
enforceable	foreign	happiness
enjoyed	foreigner	hastening
enjoyment	forfeit	hateful
enjoys	forgetful	heavily
entries	forgetting	heifer
envied	formality	height
envies	fortieth	heinous
envoys	fortifies	heir
equipment	fortunately	heiress
equipped	foxes	heiresses
equipping	freight	heirloom
Eskimos(oes)	fretful	hens
essayist	frieze	heroes
estuaries	frightened	hippopotami, -muses
excellent	fruitful	hippos
exchangeable	fulfilment	historical
exciting		hoofs *or* hooves
excitement	gaily	hoped (*from* hope)
expensive	galaxies	hoping (*from* hope)
expresses	galloped	hopped (*from* hop)
extremely	gardening	hopping (*from* hop)
	gazebos	hottest
	gipsies or gypsies	hugged
facilities	giraffes	hugging
factories	giving	hunches
faithful	glacier	hurried
fanciful	glasses	hurrying
fantasies	glorious	hutches
fastening	gossiped	hysterical
feigned	gossiping	
field	graceful	inability
fiend	grateful	inactive
fireworks	grief	inadequate
fitful	grievance	idiocies
fitness	grieve	igloos
flagstaffs	grinning	ignoble
flatly	guests	ignorance
flies	gulfs	ignored
flitted	gushes	illegal
flying	gypsies or gipsies	illegible

illiterate	labelled	magnetos
immature	labelling	manly
immediately	laboratories	making
immensely	ladies	manifestoes
immobile	laid	marketable
immortal	largely	marketing
impelled	lassos	marvellous
imperilled	lately	masses
impious	lateness	masterful
impolite	laziest	mementos, -oes
improvement	lazing	memos
inability	leafs (verb)	merciful
inadequate	learning	mien
inconclusive	leaves (noun)	miracle
incorrect	legless	mislaid
indecisive	leisure	misspelling
indefinite	levered	mixes
indirect	libraries	modified
indisputable	licence	monkeys
ineligible	licensed	mopping
informal	likable *or* likeable	mosquitoes
innuendoes	likely	mottos, -oes
instalments	liking	moving
interment	limited	moustaches
invisible	limiting	muddy
irrational	limitless	muffs
irregular	listening	musical
irrelevant	livelihood	mysteries
irreplaceable	lives	mystified
irresolute	living	
irresponsible	loaves	nautical
	lobbyist	navies
jellies	looseness	necessities
jerseys	loneliness	needed
jockeying	lonely	Negroes
jockeys	lopped	neigh
journeys	lorries	neighbour
judgment *or* judgement	losing	neither
	loveliness	nervous
kangaroos	lovely	netted
kidneys	loving	niece
kimonos	lynxes	ninth
knitted		noisily
knives	madly	noisy

noticing
numbered

oafs
obstacle
occurred
occurrence
offered
ogres
omitted
omitting
opportunities
oratorios
orbited
orbiting
ordered
outrageous
outwitted
outwitting
overcast
overcome

packeted
paid
pantos
parried
participate
participation
particle
parties
patios
patrolled
patted
paved
pays
peaceful
pedalling
penalties
penniless
peonies
perceive
permitted
petered
petrified

photos
physical
pianos
piccolos
piece
pierce
piercing
piloted
pinches
pined (*from* pine)
pining (*from* pine)
pinned (*from* pin)
pinning (*from* pin)
pitied
pitted
pivoting
planing (*from* plane)
planning (*from* plan)
played
plentiful
plied
plugged
ponchos
ponies
portfolios
portraying
portrays
potatoes
pottering
practice
practises
praising
praying
preferred
prejudices
preparations
preying
pried
priest
priggish
primly
princesses
Principal
principle

proficient
profitable
profited
proofs
propeller
prophecy
prophesy
proposed
protein
proving
pruning
prying
pulleys
punches
puppies
puritanical
pushes
putrefies
putrefying

qualified
qualifies
qualities
quantities
quarrelling
quarrelsome
quays

radios
rates
readiness
receipt
receive
received
receiving
recurrence
recurrent
reefs
reference
referring
regretful
regretted
reign

reigned
reindeer
reins
relaying
relays
relies
relieved
remorseful
repelled
replaceable
replied
replying
restful
retrieve
retriever
rimless
risottos
riveted
riveting
robbing
rodeos
roofs
rotten
rubbing
ruffs
runner

sadness
said
sandalled
satisfying
scanning
scarfs *or* scarves
scarred
scenarios
scraping
scratches
secretaries
seemed
seize
semi-circle
sentries
separately
severely

shakos
shampoos
sharing
sheafs *or* sheaves
sheaths
Sheila
shelves
sheriffs
shield
shining (*from* shine)
shinning (*from* shin)
shipped
shopped
shriek
shyly
shyness
sieve
signalled
sincerely
sinful
sinuses
sipped
sitting
skein
ski-ing
skinned
skipped
skipping
slain
slaying
sleigh
slipped
sloping (*from* slope)
slopping (*from* slop)
slyly
snapping
sniffs
snobbish
societies
soldier
sombreros
something
sometimes
sopranos

sorrowful
sovereign
species
spectacle
spiteful
spoiling
squeezing
steamer
stepped
stirred
storeys (*s.* storey)
stories (*s.* story)
studies
studios
studious
studying
submitted
submitting
sunny
supplied
supplier
supplies
supplying
surfeit
surveyor

tapped (*from* tap)
taming
tariffs
tattoos
taxes
terrifies
tests
their
themselves
thief
thieves
thinly
tiered
timing
toeing
tomatoes
topless
torpedoes

93

transmitted
traveller
travesties
trial
tricycle
tried
tries
trios
trolleys or trollies
tropical
truly
trying
tubing
turkeys
twists

umpiring
unable
uncle
uncontrolled
uncooperative
undecided
undiluted
underrate
understudies

unfair
unforgiveable
unkind
unnatural
unpredictable
unrelated
unsophisticated
untidy
useful

valleys
vanities
vein
volcanoes
volleys

waged
waging
waifs
wallabies
warring
watches
weight
weir
weird

wharfs *or* wharves
wielded
wined
wisely
wishes
wistful
witches
withhold
witnesses
wives
wolves
wonderful
wooden
worries
worshipful
worshipping
wrapped
wrenches
wryly

yield
yo-yos

zoos

Terms You Need to Know

Adjective   A 'describing' word that gives you information about a noun.

e.g. a *difficult* task.

Consonants   B C D F G H J K L M N P Q R S T V W X Y Z
All the letters of the alphabet which are not vowels.
Note: Y is a consonant at the *beginning* of a word or at the beginning of a syllable. It sounds different from y as a vowel.

e.g. yolk, yellow, beyond.
(y − consonant) = (be + yond)

Noun   The name of an object, an emotion, a place, a person, a subject, etc.

e.g. chair, happiness, Exmouth, Anna, mathematics.

Plural   Two or more of anything are said to be plural.

e.g. two loaves, three hundred boys, some houses.

Prefix   A syllable (sometimes two syllables) added to a word in the front.

e.g. MIStake, UNDERtake.

Singular   A single one of anything is said to be singular.

e.g. a loaf, one boy, a house.

Suffix   A syllable (sometimes two syllables) added to the end of a word. A consonant suffix is a suffix which begins with a consonant, and a vowel suffix is a suffix which begins with a vowel.

e.g. humourLESS, accessIBLE.

Syllable   A push of breath in the pronunciation of a word.

e.g. be   one syllable
          be-gin   two syllables
          be-hav-ing three syllables

Verb   A 'doing' word such as she *walks*, he *thinks*, they *remember*, we *munch*.

Vowels   A E I O U and sometimes Y.
Note: Y is a vowel at the *end* of words or at the *end* of syllables.

e.g. bay, muddy, boyish.
(y-vowel) = (boy + ish)

Afterword

The exercises and dictation passages in this book have given you some concentrated practice. Now you must carry on the process of improving your spelling by yourself because accuracy in spelling is maintained only by constant vigilance.

The more you read, the better your spelling will become because almost unconsciously your eyes will become used to the correct version of words. Learn too to read your own work analytically. Carefully check all written work before handing it in, ensuring that there are no obvious spelling mistakes. When your work is returned, take care to note the corrections that have been made. You will see then the errors that you *missed* when you thought you were checking your work. Enter correct spellings in your alphabetical notebook so that the words can be easily located next time.

Remember that if you find a word particularly difficult to learn, it can be attacked from more than one direction. Try writing it again and again so that your hand guides your brain. Try spelling it aloud so that you will be able to remember your voice and its emphasis. Try writing it on a piece of paper and pinning it on the wall so that you keep seeing it unexpectedly. Your eye will gradually assimilate the correct order of the letters.

Your first step is to discover which words you can't spell. Your second step is to make sure you know where to find the correct versions of these words quickly when you need them (your notebook). Your third step is to learn these words so thoroughly that they will never trouble you again.

Gradually your personal 'pool' of errors will be reduced. You will be winning!